PEARSON
His Life and World

FRONTISPIECE
Lester Bowles Pearson: the
official portrait in the
Parliament Buildings,
Ottawa, by Hugh Mac-
Kenzie.
*Reproduced by permission
of the Sergeant-at-Arms,
Parliament Buildings,
Ottawa. Photography by
John Evans, Ottawa.*

ROBERT BOTHWELL

PEARSON
His Life and World

General Editor: W. Kaye Lamb

Picture Editor: Paul Russell

McGraw-Hill Ryerson Limited

Toronto Montreal New York London

PEARSON: HIS LIFE AND WORLD
Copyright © McGraw-Hill Ryerson Limited, 1978.
    All rights reserved. No part of this publication may be reproduced, stored
in a retrieval system, or transmitted, in any form, or by any means, electronic,
mechanical, photocopying, recording, or otherwise, without the prior written
permission of McGraw-Hill Ryerson Limited.

ISBN   0-07-082305-7

1 2 3 4 5 6 7 8 9 10 BP 7 6 5 4 3 2 1 0 9 8

Printed and bound in Canada

Canadian Cataloguing in Publication Data

Bothwell, Robert, date
    Pearson

(Prime Ministers of Canada)

Bibliography: p.
Includes index.
ISBN 0-07-082305-7

1. Pearson, Lester B., 1897-1972. 2. Prime ministers — Canada — Biography.
3. Canada — Politics and government — 1963-   * I. Series.

FC621.P4B68   971.06'43'0924   C78-001210-0
F1034.3.P4B68

Contents

TO HEATHER

The Pearson family about
1900, when Lester
(standing on the chair
beside his mother) was
three.
*Public Archives Canada,
C-18704.*

1
The Loose-
Jointed Diplomat

ON THE SIXTH of August, 1945, the Prime Minister of Canada rose to address a dominion-provincial conference. "I told those present that I had an earth-shaking announcement to make," Mackenzie King later wrote in his diary. "I then mentioned in a word the dropping of the atomic bomb."

On February 5, 1968, the Prime Minister of Canada stood up to welcome delegates to yet another dominion-provincial conference, although, in deference to changing times, it was now called a federal-provincial conference. While the names had changed, the essential subject of the conference had not: how was the great, sprawling country of Canada to be governed, and by whom? From the age of Mackenzie King to the age of Lester Pearson it had not been far if distance is measured in chronological or even constitutional terms. But if the yardstick is that of the atomic age, then Canada had come a long way indeed.

Lester Pearson's life, like the history of Canada, was made up of paradoxes. A professional diplomat, he became a successful professional politician. Outwardly modest and engaging, he nevertheless achieved ambitions beyond the wildest dreams of a boy born in suburban Toronto in the year of Queen

Victoria's Diamond Jubilee. Like most Canadians, he saw his country's horizons simultaneously widen and contract in the course of a single lifetime.

Circa 1898.
Public Archives Canada,
C-22539.

To begin with it all looked very simple. Lester Bowles Pearson was born the son of a Methodist parson in Newtonbrook, Ontario, on April 23, 1897. His country and his world were well-defined. Canada was a part, a large and important part to be sure, of the great world-wide British Empire, over which Queen Victoria had been presiding for almost sixty years. In Canada, of course, the actual government was entrusted to a cabinet responsible to a duly elected Parliament, while a British aristocrat represented the Queen as Governor General. The effective leader of the country was the Prime Minister, Mr. Wilfrid Laurier, soon to become Sir Wilfrid, the silver-tongued orator from Quebec. According to Laurier,

the fast-approaching twentieth century would belong to Canada.

Laurier's verbal extravaganza expressed the mood of his times: confident, self-assured, progressive. Progress, guided no doubt, by Laurier's Liberal party, would be good to Canada in terms of material development. As for spiritual development, that was less the concern of the state, even the liberal state, than the duty of the churches and the home. These sound institutions were strong and certain. Methodism, the ruling creed in most of rural Ontario, stressed the simple, homely virtues, which included patriotism and a stern code of personal good conduct. It also preached a vision of a better society, towards which good Christians should strive.

On the children's level, Methodism meant a combination of homely precepts and godly virtues against the most obvious of society's ills: liquor, tobacco, and gambling, which of course included cards. In the course of an active diplomatic life the pledge against liquor, at least, had to be dispensed with. But by the end of Pearson's life God was no longer a Methodist, but rather He had merged with the Presbyterians and the Congregationalists and had become United.

Pearson worked hard in school, and became one of the minority of high school graduates who went on to university. By the time he entered Victoria College, the Methodist college in the University of Toronto, it was the fall of 1913. Sir Wilfrid Laurier was no longer Prime Minister, and Sir Robert Borden presided over the financial problems that had resulted from Sir Wilfrid's incurable optimism. These governmental affairs had little impact on the cheerful life of a university student, and when Pearson's first year drew to a successful close in the spring of 1914, there was little reason to believe that they ever would.

That summer was spent in Chatham, Ontario, where the Pearson family had moved to still another parsonage. Pearson strengthened his ball-playing skills as second base for one of the local teams. In the middle of the season, as he long after recalled, "my world ended, though I did not know it for some months." On August 4, 1914, Great Britain declared war on the German Empire.

The causes of the war were lost in Balkan politics, never the centre of interest in Canadian homes. If Britain was in, it must be important, but in all likelihood the war would be over in six months. The war was still on when Pearson returned to college in September. In October, the First Canadian Division sailed down the St. Lawrence for Europe. More troops fol-

13

Tyranny of the Corner, Sashay Set, by Harold Town (1962). Town was the leading figure in Painters Eleven, the Toronto group that in 1954 held the first exhibition of completely abstract and non-objective art held in the city. A worker in many media — paintings, silk screens, collages and sculpture — he is a showman as well as an artist and is much in the public eye. Firmly wedded to Toronto, he has seldom left that city. *The National Gallery of Canada, Ottawa.*

At a fishing camp in Wisconsin in 1920, to which Pearson had escaped briefly from his servitude in Chicago with the Armour Fertilizer works.
Public Archives Canada, PA-110827.

In External Affairs Pearson became part of a small but elite group of young diplomats. For the most part, the calibre of the Canadian foreign service created by Dr. Skelton was extraordinarily high, stocked with talented lawyers, professors, and poets manqués. Pearson and his contemporaries, Norman Robertson, Hume Wrong and Hugh Keenleyside, as well as some later appointments like Jack Pickersgill and Charles Ritchie, gave a distinct lustre to the hitherto rather humdrum Canadian public service.

Pearson's particular friends were Robertson and Wrong, and the three men remained close throughout their lives. Wrong had been a lecturer in history at Toronto, like Pearson, where he made a reputation for brilliance. This reputation was expanded in the civil service. Wrong would not suffer fools

gladly, and his manner occasionally indicated to Mackenzie King that the Prime Minister was one of the number. Wrong's career was accordingly punctuated by confrontations with one or the other of his masters, and he poured out his lamentations to his friends. Robertson soon established a solid reputation for intelligence, integrity and competence that took him far above the ordinary run of civil servants.

Perseverance and patience were also essential qualities. Junior diplomats served their apprenticeship clipping newspapers, reading back files, running errands for the Prime Minister (who was also Minister of External Affairs), and writing endless memoranda for Dr. Skelton. These memoranda, painstaking, idealistic and largely fruitless, were the epitaph of this generation. Pearson's were exceptional, even among his

Playing with the Oxford hockey team in Murren, Switzerland, in 1921. *Public Archives Canada, PA-119892.*

The Pearsons' double wedding, August 22, 1925: Grace Moody and Norman Young on the left; Maryon Moody and Lester Pearson on the right.
Public Archives Canada, PA-68799.

talented peers. Humorous, on occasion incisive, clear in thought and prose, they belied Massey's "loose-jointed" description.

Service in Ottawa was swiftly followed by posting to the field. Pearson's first assignment was to Herbert Hoover's Washington in the summer of 1929. Washington was then a quiet, if uncomfortable, place to be. There was little enough to do, and virtually nothing to report on. When cooler weather brought the regular legation staff back to Washington, Pearson returned to Ottawa. His next mission was to the London Naval Conference of January 1930. Canada's presence was

more a matter of courtesy than urgency— the Canadian navy
with its three small ships would have been imperilled by any
cuts that could not be resolved in thirds. In fact, as it proved,
the agenda of the conference was less important than the experience, social and diplomatic, gained in the process. London
was still very much the centre of the British Empire, which
was only very slowly coming to be called the British Commonwealth. Most events of international significance had a British
dimension, and most Canadians expected their government, on
important matters, to follow the British lead. Mackenzie King
did not fully share this opinion (and Dr. Skelton did not share

Pearson (second from right) attending his first important international meeting—the London Naval Disarmament Conference of 1930. On his right is Col. J. L. Ralston, then Minister of National Defence.
Public Archives Canada, PA-25146.

it at all), but in a peaceful decade the question of effective autonomy was academic.

By January 1930 Mackenzie King was not long for the prime ministership. He was defeated and replaced in August by the Conservative leader, R. B. Bennett. Although Pearson's own political beliefs were evolving away from "British-Conservative" by this time, he found this no impediment to cordial relations with Bennett. Bennett used External Affairs, as King had, as a reservoir of talent and advice for widely varying tasks. Pearson found himself Secretary to the Royal Commission on Price Spreads and followed the Commissioners as they traversed the country investigating industrial conditions

in the depths of the great depression. While working for the Commission he met and befriended a young Toronto accountant, Walter L. Gordon. Gordon later described Pearson's "good humour, hard work and tact" in a difficult job, qualities for which, Gordon added, "he was already becoming known."

For the most part, however, Pearson worked steadily in his proper role as foreign service officer. In 1932 he visited Geneva, seat of the League of Nations, as part of the Canadian delegation to a world disarmament conference. The League of Nations, under the shadow of world economic collapse, and with international storm signs flying, was making a brave, forlorn effort to get the nations of the world to disarm before it was too late. Canada was virtually disarmed. Its troops' principal duty in the early 1930s was to run relief camps for the unemployed. Canada could, however, contribute verbal support to international peace and disarmament, and in

Pearson with Dr. O. D. Skelton on board the *Berengaria* in 1933. Skelton, Undersecretary of State for External Affairs from 1925 until his death in 1941, was the man who brought Pearson into the Canadian foreign service. *Public Archives Canada, PA-110825.*

The Royal Commission on Price Spreads of 1934, which Pearson (seated, sixth from the left) served as Secretary. He had already acted as Secretary of a Royal Commission on Grain Futures. *Public Archives Canada, PA-51536.*

the meantime, provide diplomatic assistance to the larger purposes of British diplomacy. Once again, however, Pearson found himself participating in an exercise in futility. "Canada is not an important member of the League," R. B. Bennett wrote in 1933, and Canadian views on disarmament held no interest for European governments. In that same year, 1933, the new German government led by Adolf Hitler walked out of the conference and out of the League.

Pearson's generation had already gone through the searing experience of the First World War. Some clung to the belief, officially embodied in the League of Nations, that peace was indivisible, and that only through "collective security" and mutual support could the world hope to escape another round of militarism, aggression, and war. Others, however, derived the lesson that great power diplomacy and power politics (including efforts towards collective security), were discredited and discreditable, that ideology was relative, and that there could be no such thing as absolute good or evil in the world.

Pearson had a front seat for the events of the 1930s. In 1935 he was posted to the Canadian High Commission in London as first secretary (but third in command) to Vincent Massey. In London, Pearson could contemplate the increasingly desperate efforts of the British government to make a lasting, stable peace on the European continent, and which was operating on the principle that nothing could be more dreadful than war. This meant accommodation with Hitler's Germany

— "appeasement," if it could be achieved. It also meant compromise with the fascist government of Italy under Benito Mussolini.

In the fall of 1935 Mussolini, at that time an ally of Britain and France, invaded the independent African empire of Ethiopia. He expected the British and French to turn a blind eye, in return for his support against Germany. An outraged public opinion in Britain demanded that their government take action against Mussolini. Those who, like Pearson, believed in resistance to aggression, in collective security, rallied round the League, which roused itself to a last desperate effort to save the world from a general calamity. On the motion of Canada's delegate to the League, oil sanctions, which if universally applied would have cut off oil to Italy and brought the mechanized Italian army to a dusty halt, were approved in Geneva. Pearson, who was working with the Canadian delegation to the League, was relieved and encouraged. But in December the Canadian government, once again under Mackenzie King, ordered the repudiation of oil sanctions. Pearson was forced to spend his Christmas vacation shuttling back and forth between London and Geneva carrying out the distasteful task of insuring a Canadian presence at meetings where it was well

An interesting photograph of Pearson at Canada House, in London, in 1936. Vincent Massey, then High Commissioner, is seated on the right; Georges P. Vanier, Secretary to the High Commissioner, is on the left. Ross McLean, attaché, stands beside Pearson. None of those in the picture can have suspected that the group included two future Governors General and a future Prime Minister of Canada. *Public Archives Canada, C-4053.*

27

known that Canada had nothing to contribute. To make matters worse, if possible, the British government had reneged on its support of the League and had offered Mussolini most of what he wanted.

In the summer of 1936 sanctions were ignominiously rescinded by the League and Ethiopia became another colony in Italy's African empire. Mussolini promptly signed an alliance with Hitler.

The performance of the British government in this episode had been discouraging in the extreme. Negotiating from weakness, it consistently gave away its hand and emerged from each confrontation more bereft of allies and more discredited in reputation. It was a disheartening spectacle for Pearson. When British appeasement of Germany was climaxed by the surrender of part of Czechoslovakia in the Munich Conference, Pearson saw clearly that this was only a reprieve. One of his letters home to Dr. Skelton catches clearly the flavour of the times:

> With a somnambulist in Berlin, a ruthless blood-and-iron tyrant in Rome, a frightened crowd of politicians in Paris, and confusion and uncertainty in London, what hope can there be for peace and order? I hope my presumption will be pardoned when I say that if I were responsible for Canadian policy, I would assume that war in Europe is certain within five years, that [Britain] acting in my opinion more by instinct than by reason, will slide into the mess, and that, in view of the bloody chaos that will result, our chief interest now is to avoid being involved in any circumstances.

Dr. Skelton needed no convincing on that score. Right up to September 1939, he urged Mackenzie King to keep Canada out of a European war.

Pearson's views were not so consistent. By the time the final crisis arrived, in August 1939, he had decided that his instincts lay with the British, who with all their faults still stood for decency and order, and against the "savagery and barbarism" represented by the other side. In that month, Pearson was back in Canada on vacation. Cutting his vacation short, he persuaded Skelton to let him fly back to his post (a trans-Atlantic flight was still a notable adventure), where he arrived in time for the German invasion of Poland on September 1. Britain declared war on Germany on September 3, and Canada followed on September 10.

The show of determination signalled by the declarations of war was not matched by the purposeful prosecution of the

British or Canadian war efforts. For the first eight months of the war, Neville Chamberlain, the apostle of appeasement, was still Britain's Prime Minister — "an obstinate old man of limited vision," Pearson wrote, adding prophetically, "and, I believe, with a limited tenure of office."

Back on the Canadian side of the Atlantic, the Canadian government made haste slowly, preoccupied by the magnitude of the costs of the war, and distracted by political battles on the home front. Nonetheless, within weeks a decision was made to send Canadian troops overseas and in December 1939 Canada's first division landed in the British Isles, to finish its training and complete its equipment. Both were incomplete when the Germans defeated the British and French armies on the continent and overran France. Britain and the Commonwealth fought on alone. In England, Churchill was now Prime Minister — "a step in the right direction," in Pearson's opinion.

With the battle of France over, the Battle of Britain began. Hitler sent his air force to soften up British defences prior to the expected invasion. But the German air force was not strong enough or skilful enough to defeat the British in the air, nor could it succeed in aerial bombardment. The British endured constant German air attacks during the fall and winter of 1940. Pearson remained in London, which was

The "Hudson" engine used on the Royal Tour of 1939. The spotty history of the railways was to have an additional episode from the fifties on when passengers began to desert to airlines and buses.
Corporate Archives, Canadian Pacific.

one of the Germans' principal targets, and suffered the uncertainties and privations faced by the rest of the civilian population. Since he was on the spot, he was called on to gratify one of Mackenzie King's more peculiar instructions to his harassed foreign service. The Prime Minister had learned that Westminster Hall had been bombed, and decided that some of the fragments would make a splendid addition to his own private collection of ruins at his country estate of Kingsmere. He ordered Pearson to procure some of the rubble, and to send it on to King in Canada. A surprised British Office of Works complied with Pearson's strange request, and the stones survived the hazards of submarine warfare to come to rest at Kingsmere.

Pearson's stay in London was cut short by a series of deaths in the Canadian foreign service. In January 1941 Dr. Skelton collapsed and died at the wheel of his car in Ottawa. Simultaneously the Canadian minister in Washington, Loring Christie, also a senior diplomat, became mortally ill. An immediate replacement seemed necessary, and Norman Robertson got the nod for the undersecretary's job, while Leighton McCarthy, a prominent Liberal from Toronto and friend of American President Roosevelt, was sent to Washington.

Pearson had wanted, and expected, Skelton's position, and had he been in Ottawa, as Robertson wrote, he would have succeeded as undersecretary. Under the circumstances, Pearson swallowed his disappointment and loyally supported his friend. He returned to Ottawa to assist Robertson, while Hume Wrong was sent to Washington to help McCarthy. When Wrong and McCarthy proved incompatible, Pearson went to Washington instead.

Washington in the spring of 1942 was the heart, if not the soul, of the allied war effort. The Americans had only been officially in the war since the previous December, but for over a year American money and munitions had been sustaining Britain and its allies. President Roosevelt and Winston Churchill, fortunately, got along famously, and the direction of the war was a cordially, and jointly, run thing. Canada, in these circumstances, was sometimes treated as the ghost at the feast, and it was an important part of the responsibilities of Canadian diplomats to make certain that Canada received due recognition, and consultation, when and where required.

The British were used to this by now, but the Americans were not. Canadian diplomacy often ran up against a wall of baffled incomprehension, even though the American be-

Meanwhile Pearson had advanced considerably in rank. On January 1, 1945, he took McCarthy's place as Canadian Ambassador to the United States (there had been a change of title in 1944), and presented his credentials to President Roosevelt shortly before the latter's death. His mission to Washington was widely praised as a great success, and he had favourably impressed Mackenzie King. He had made a good impression on others as well, and when the new United Nations got under way, Pearson was suggested as the first Secretary General. The Soviet Union objected, and Pearson lost his chance for that particular distinction. Instead, in the summer of 1946, he was informed that he was to return to Ottawa as Robertson's replacement in Dr. Skelton's chair.

The Canadian delegation at the founding conference of the United Nations in San Francisco in 1945. Mackenzie King, the Prime Minister, is at the head of the table; Mr. St. Laurent is on his right. Pearson is leaning forward, head on hand.
Public Archives Canada, C-22719.

2
The New Nationalism

Viscount Alexander, the Governor General, signing the bill that provided for the admission of Newfoundland to Canada in 1949. Prime Minister St. Laurent is on his right, and the Speakers of the Senate and House of Commons are on his left.
Public Archives Canada, C-21401.

"As PEARSON came into the office, I was struck by his fine face and appearance," Mackenzie King wrote. "There was a light which shone through his countenance." It was no small wonder why Pearson had, at age forty-nine, reached the top of his profession. He was not the youngest man to be under-secretary of state for external affairs (both Skelton and Robertson had been younger when appointed), but his youth-ful appearance and vivacity belied his middle age. Instead of Skelton's and Robertson's dour public gravity, there was Pear-son's grin, his bow tie, his easy and friendly manner, sym-bolized by his nickname, "Mike." It was a popular appointment.

Yet apart from a few friends and family, very few knew the man behind the bow tie. It is doubtful that his "public and private personalities were one and the same," as one reporter wrote, and Pearson's passport to success was his ability to make this appear to be so. Perhaps, with time, the public manner increasingly overlaid the private man, freezing what had been natural into a stylized bonhomie which concealed what it seemed to open. Arnold Heeney, a close friend, wrote of the mature Pearson that "over the years, although con-sistently friendly and satisfactory with me, he is increasingly impersonal – a deep one whose secret self very few, if any can know."

This was not the Mike Pearson the public knew, nor the candid and vigorous diplomat his colleagues knew and re-spected. In his own way, Pearson was coming to resemble the man who was now his direct boss, Mackenzie King. Much later, one of his cabinet colleagues tried to sum up Pearson by calling him "a nice Mackenzie King." In political skills as well as secretiveness Pearson was learning from the old master.

As yet, however, Pearson had a lot to learn, or re-learn, about Canada. He had been out of the country for over a decade, with only a brief stay in 1941-42 to vary his foreign experience. He knew, far better than most Canadians, what kind of a world Canada had to get along in. But he knew com-paratively little about the country that he had been repre-senting. When Pearson left Ottawa in 1935 it was the sleepy capital of a country in the throes of a desperate economic depression. When he returned in 1946, it was to a larger city thronging with civil servants housed in uncomfortable clap-board temporary buildings, constructed to serve the wartime emergency. The temporary buildings were still there, and so was the emergency.

The experience of war was fresh, but behind it lay the memory of the depression and of the inability of the govern-

ments of the 1930s to meet the emergency of economic collapse. During the depression, provincial sovereignty had been an insurmountable barrier to efforts to deal with the economy in a co-ordinated way, but during the war Canada's "emergency constitution," sanctioned by the British North America Act, came into effect. This alternate constitution concentrated all power in the hands of the central government for the duration of the wartime emergency. It was the national government that had fought and won the war for Canada, that had taxed, spent, employed on an unprecedented scale. Central planning for the Canadian economy had arrived along with controls. For the duration, the provinces had become pensioners of the central government, receiving financial equivalents for the surrender of their tax revenues. This system, embodied in the Wartime Tax Agreements, was the centrepiece of the new Liberal federalism.

Wellington Street, Ottawa, west of the Supreme Court building, as it was at the close of the Second World War. This conglomeration of old brick houses and business blocks and temporary wooden office buildings hastily built during the war has now given way to imposing new government buildings. The Garden of the Provinces would be in the middle of an up-to-date photograph.
National Capital Commission.

The Camouflaged Piano or *French Roundels*, by Greg Curnoe (1966). Curnoe was born in London, Ontario, and has spent most of his life there. In his approach to both life and painting he has rejected established ways. He founded a Nihilist Party and organized a Nihilist Spasm Band with kazoos. His painting of Victoria Hospital, London, which was bought by the National Gallery of Canada, is painted in oil, latex and mixed media on plywood, with marking ink, iron mesh and wallpaper added. In 1976 eight of his paintings were chosen to represent Canada at the International Biennial art exhibition in Venice; each was a view from a different window in his London studio. *The Camouflaged Piano* is a mixture of themes rather than media; probably only the artist himself could explain its meaning.

The National Gallery of Canada, Ottawa.

Confedespread, by Joyce Wieland (1967). Her work well illustrates the ferment and rejection of convention characteristic of the contemporary art world. She has moved from medium to medium, breaking down the divisions between them and bringing them together in combinations that often appear bizarre. She has been a film maker; and she has produced paintings in which whole series of shots from film appear. She made a quilted bedspread for a friend, and from this came the idea of quilted wall hangings. Many of these are large and complicated; *Arctic Day* consists of 160 pincushions, each bearing a drawing of northern flora or fauna. *Confedespread* may look like a painting in the photograph, but it is actually composed of plastic compartments filled with flags and shag, and was a salute to confederation and Expo 67.
The National Gallery of Canada, Ottawa.

Canadians were pleased with the way the war had been run on the economic front. Economic controls had been annoying, and the strict regulation of production, distribution, wages and prices by Ottawa had occasionally been unpopular. Nevertheless, the system had worked. It was hoped that the

same might be done after the war, but there was considerable worry about the government's ability to muster the same forces in peacetime that it had harnessed in war.

Mackenzie King had sensed the turn in public opinion. In 1944 the Liberals enacted family allowances, providing a monthly sum to every child in the country through cheques issued from Ottawa. Civil servants were set to work on a comprehensive anti-unemployment package that could guarantee to the nation that the thirties would never return. The result of their labours was incorporated in a "Green Book" of federal proposals and presented to a dominion-provincial conference in August 1945.

The Liberal government's proposals called for the centralization of most of the country's financial authority in Ottawa. The provinces, in return, were to get equalization grants that would help to correct the disparity in levels of government services from coast to coast. The concentration of control over Canada's financial resources in Ottawa was justified by the necessity to control the economy as it had not been controlled in the thirties. This could only be done by a truly sizeable federal budget, which would be "the balance wheel of the economy." In addition, the government proposed to adopt a series of social welfare measures, including comprehensive health insurance for all.

King regarded the dominion-provincial conference as a very fragile instrument of government. It was too easy for something to go wrong. An objection from one or the other of the major provinces would be enough to finish matters, and objections did come. Ontario and Quebec in particular objected to losing their autonomy in the manner prescribed by the federal proposals. Premier Duplessis of Quebec unkindly compared the federal proposals to the political theories of Hitler and Mussolini, while Drew of Ontario "literally boomed defiance" in what a British diplomat called a "verbose and diffuse statement." The conference collapsed, and Drew and Duplessis returned to their respective capitals breathing hatred at the wicked centralizers in Ottawa.

Despite the apparent failure of the government's proposals, the Green Book had an importance beyond 1945. The comprehensive financial and social security arrangements that it urged would eventually find friends, even in Ontario and Quebec. The central government managed, despite the conference, to retain a much greater role in the direction of the Canadian economy than it had ever possessed before, and health insurance, greater unemployment insurance benefits,

OPPOSITE
Douglas Abbott, Minister of Finance in the first five years of the St. Laurent ministry, when balanced budgets and reductions in the national debt were the order of the day.
Public Archives Canada, C-81450.

43

and more old age pensions became watchwords in Canadian politics over the next generation. For many items in the Green Book program it would be necessary to wait twenty years, until the Pearson government found the resources and the political support for implementing them.

The Green Book and the economic concepts that inspired it provided a framework for the policies followed by the federal Liberals after 1945. In that year, the Liberals had been in power for a decade. When the war ended, King called a general election and scraped through with a bare majority in the House of Commons, though losing his own seat in the process. A safe seat was swiftly provided so that King could attend the new Parliament and confront the new Opposition Leader, the Conservatives' John Bracken, in the fall of 1945.

At his back King had the Liberal party. That the party had survived the war intact was due in no small part to King's phenomenal political skill in handling the potentially divisive issue of conscription, and in reconciling Quebec to its eventual imposition. King's reward came in the 1945 election when the Liberals once again swept a "solid Quebec" against minor and scattered opposition. The end of the war had deprived the nationalists of an issue, and with conscription gone, who could replace Père King? In both French and English Canada King had survived most of his contemporaries and colleagues, inside and outside the party. His ministers in 1945 were a younger generation, men who had not grown up in the memory of William Lyon Mackenzie, or ripened in the shadow of Laurier. They were men like C. D. Howe, who had run Canada's war production during the recent conflict, and who was now in charge of the government's reconstruction program, and Louis St. Laurent, the Minister of Justice who had helped keep Quebec in the fold in the darkest hours of the war. Beneath them was another, still younger generation: Brooke Claxton, the highly successful Minister of Health and Welfare in charge of the new program of family allowances; Douglas Abbott, who was about to become Minister of Finance; Paul Martin and Lionel Chevrier, two Franco-Ontarians who balanced the Anglo-Quebeckers, Abbott and Claxton, in the cabinet. These men were Pearson's friends and contemporaries, as well as his potential rivals. Together they made up a truly formidable political and administrative team.

It was well that the government was as strong as it was. King, the leader, turned seventy-one in 1945. Although his iron constitution had stood up well under the rigours of war, his strength was finally beginning to flag. A trip to Europe

45

One of the worst Canadian disasters of the Pearson era occurred late on a September night in 1949 when the cruise ship *Noronic* burned at her dock in Toronto Harbour. Over a hundred passengers lost their lives. Some compensation came with changes in shipboard fire prevention regulations that made a repetition of the disaster unlikely. *City of Toronto Archives, James Collection #1518.*

in the summer of 1946 to attend the Paris Peace Conference produced no improvement. A tired and cranky Prime Minister tore strips off his staff on the trip home, all except Pearson. "I like Pearson exceedingly," King wrote in his diary of the trip. "I feel sure his judgment will be helpful in the working out of what is best for all concerned."

What was best for Mackenzie King, the Prime Minister decided, was the reduction of his work load. Accordingly, he summoned Louis St. Laurent and asked him to take over as Minister of External Affairs. When Pearson returned to Ottawa in September 1946 he found that he had a new chief, the first man since Sir Robert Borden not to be Prime Minister and Minister of External Affairs at the same time. King had his eye on both Pearson and St. Laurent, and his gaze was not purely paternal.

Throughout his career King had given more than passing thought to the question of his successor. St. Laurent wished to bow out of federal politics at the end of the war and return to his law practice, but at King's request the day of his departure kept receding. His move to external affairs was intended to be temporary, an expedient to help King out of a jam. But the temporary posting became permanent in December. In spite of occasional minor differences, King had come to find

St. Laurent indispensable in the cabinet, and believed that the Minister of External Affairs was the man to succeed him as leader of the Liberal party. In July 1947 he told St. Laurent so, and after considerable persuasion, St. Laurent agreed to run.

It was no light decision. St. Laurent was already sixty-five. He had a distinguished career behind him: successful lawyer, batonnier of the Quebec bar, President of the Canadian Bar Association, and finally, Minister of Justice. He was, as his colleague Brooke Claxton later wrote, a "strangely simple man," "honest and humble," and felt no compulsion to pursue the highest political office.

With St. Laurent moving to the Prime Minister's Office, the question arose of a possible successor, in external affairs. In King's opinion, Pearson was the proper choice. When Pearson became undersecretary he knew that King had it in mind that he might get "into public life here." And when, in late 1946, King discussed the leadership question with a sympathetic newsman, both agreed that Pearson would be an admirable political acquisition, and in the distant future might well become "the best of any successor" to King himself. "This," King wrote, "is something which only the future can settle and in the circumstances and the times which would make anything of the kind possible."

The long wait began. King told the cabinet at the end of July 1947 that he expected to retire in the coming year and that they must give thought to a convention to choose a successor. But King was still very much Prime Minister, and he could still exercise his authority when he chose. This was particularly the case with external affairs, which he viewed as his special preserve. King was also obsessed with what he considered to be the lessons of the past, and his direct memory of the past stretched all the way back to the 1890s.

Pearson and St. Laurent had found that they made a good team in external affairs. St. Laurent had every confidence in his deputy. Unlike King, he could grasp a situation quickly, and where a decision was required it was not postponed. Moreover, St. Laurent believed in the delegation of authority, something that King had avoided wherever possible in foreign affairs.

Canada's foreign policy, in the late 1940s, was to support the United Nations in its endeavours, and to co-operate with the United States and the United Kingdom, wherever possible or expedient. Support for the UN was predicated less on a fervent appreciation of the way in which the international body functioned than on a resigned feeling that no better

Messengers Juggling Seeds, by Jack Chambers (1962). This painting was executed shortly after Chambers returned from Spain, where he spent nine years, to his native London, Ontario. Scenes in and around London soon became his chief interest. A painting of London's Victoria Hospital, in which he was born, gained him notoriety when it was sold for $35 000 — at the time, the highest price ever paid to a Canadian painter for a single work.
The National Gallery of Canada, Ottawa.

prospect was in sight. The UN had to be kept going, no matter what disappointment its conduct might cause. By 1947 the UN had become the focus for the diplomatic duel between the western powers on the one hand and the Soviet Union and its followers on the other. The United States effectively controlled a majority of the General Assembly, and UN commissions and committees tended to agree with the American position on most matters.

By 1947 the United States wanted to find a way to get its occupying forces out of Korea. The best way of procuring this seemed to be the setting up of a UN commission to supervise elections for a successor government, the first independent Korean government since that country's annexation by Japan in 1910. The only problem was that the United States occupied only the southern half of the country, below the 38th parallel. The Russians occupied the north. The Russian idea of a proper successor government differed from the Americans'. When the Americans asked the Canadian delegation at the UN to agree to Canada's inclusion on the UN commission Pearson agreed, and so advised the head of Canada's UN delegation, the Minister of Justice, J. L. Ilsley. Ilsley reluctantly gave his consent. There the matter rested. It seemed like a routine nomination to an ordinary UN committee, and Pearson treated it as such.

In the course of time a Canadian was nominated to the commission, and the nomination came before the cabinet. There, Mackenzie King, in the recollection of Brooke Claxton, now Minister of National Defence, "blew a gasket." King believed that the situation in the Far East was far more serious than did St. Laurent. He feared that an international incident might develop out of which incalculable consequences, perhaps even war, might flow. King proceeded to lecture St. Laurent "as if he was a naughty little school-boy who had committed a sin against the Holy Ghost." St. Laurent controlled his temper "with noticeable difficulty," and agreed to investigate the situation. At the next cabinet meeting an impasse developed. King refused to authorize a Canadian representative for the United Nations Commission, and Ilsley and St. Laurent contemplated resignation. King instructed St. Laurent to find some way out of the commission for Canada. This could only be done with American consent, and so Pearson was dispatched to Washington to tell the amazed Americans that Canada would not, after all, serve on the commission. His mission was unproductive. The Americans could not understand why King was making such a fuss about an essentially trivial matter. Their reply did not convince King, who remained determined to repudiate Ilsley's action. If this happened, Ilsley, St. Laurent, and possibly others would resign. When Pearson discussed the situation with St. Laurent he wondered aloud whether his own resignation was not called for, under the circumstances. St. Laurent and King made one last effort to reach a compromise. The occasion was well-chosen: a good dinner. A solution was decided upon. A Canadian would be appointed, but he would withdraw from the commission if the Russians obstructed its work. The most improbable cabinet crisis in Canadian history ended happily, with a compromise on the issue designed to save King's face. Face was the essence. As Claxton put it, "these were the last bellows of the leader of the herd before he cashed in his cheques." Pearson said the same thing, but more sedately: "He may be merely attempting to re-establish a position in the cabinet which has been slipping as the day comes for his retirement."

There were more urgent matters claiming the attention of the cabinet and the undersecretary. After the war Canada's trade with Europe had not been re-established. The Europeans, including the British, were short of American dollars, which Canada needed to pay for imports from the United States. Late in 1947 Canadian reserves of US dollars declined at an alarming rate, and finance minister Abbott imposed severe controls to stem the outward flow. The incident pointed up the weakness of Canada's international trading position at a time when it seemed that Europe would never fully recover from the devastation of the war. In the opinion of some Canadian and American officials, the solution was a free trade agreement between Canada and the United States. The American government favoured the plan.

Initially, so did Mackenzie King, but after due consideration, he rejected it. The political implications were too hard to swallow. However convenient economic integration might be in the short run, in the longer term it would lead to the absorption of Canada by the United States and the disruption of the British Commonwealth. King could remember Laurier's defeat over reciprocity in 1911, and he did not wish to witness a second debacle. When King informed his officials, they were naturally disappointed, a fact which confirmed the Prime Minister's opinion that he was right. Canadian officials, in his opinion, were far too likely to be misled by the Americans with flattery and false promises.

Reciprocity with the United States was not forgotten, but it was merely postponed until King left office. Pearson brought

it up again in 1949 when St. Laurent visited the United States, and argued that it was still a project which Canada ought to consider seriously. St. Laurent evidently did not agree, and there the matter rested.

Another external affairs dream had a happier ending. When Canada had been formed in 1867, other segments of British North America had remained aloof. Over the course of the next several decades these had been absorbed into Canada until by 1880, when the Arctic islands were acquired, only Newfoundland remained aloof, an independent, self-governing colony. In 1933 Newfoundland had been forced by the depression and bankruptcy to give up self-government and to turn once more to direct rule from Britain. During the Second World War, Canada had assumed responsibility for Newfoundland's defence, but under an Anglo-American

Barbara Ann Scott, born in Ottawa in 1928, turned professional after her Olympic victory in 1948. Her international triumphs were a matter of pride for Canadians across the country.
Newfoundland Archives.

agreement, American troops were stationed there as well. With the end of the war it was obvious that Newfoundland would recover self-government in the near future. The question was, whether Newfoundland would return to its earlier status as a self-governing, autonomous unit inside the British Commonwealth, or associate itself with the United States, or, just possibly, become a province of Canada.

The last alternative strongly appealed to a Newfoundland broadcaster and failed pig farmer named Joseph R. (Joey) Smallwood. Using his wits and his considerable oratorical skills, Smallwood created a pro-Confederation movement, procured money from Liberal supporters in Canada, and squeaked through to victory in a referendum in July 1948. The margin was slim, and it was doubtful that Mackenzie King would accept the result of such a narrow victory. His secretary, Jack Pickersgill, found the solution by informing King that the result in Newfoundland was better than King's own percentage of the popular vote in any Canadian election. Canada acquired its tenth province, and the Liberal party acquired a new and enthusiastic recruit in Smallwood, who became premier of the new province.

At about the same time the Canadian Liberal party received another, rather less fervent member. To no-one's very great surprise, Pearson resigned from the civil service and was appointed Minister of External Affairs in succession to St. Laurent, who was finally about to take over from Mackenzie King. King's time had finally run out, although he held on for another month. Pearson became the last recruit to the cabinet of a man who, forty years before, had himself resigned from the civil service to seek a ministerial career.

As usual on such occasions, King expressed great satisfaction with his new prize. Pearson, he told his colleagues, "would be a strength in the Government." To Pearson, he predicted that "some day he would be holding the office which I was holding at the present time."

The first requirement of a minister was of course that he be appointed; the second that he (for there were as yet no women in the cabinet) become a member of one or the other of the Houses of Parliament. In Pearson's case, Tom Farquhar, the member for Algoma East, sacrificed his seat in return for a senatorship. Pearson contested the vacancy under Senator Farquhar's tutelage. He instructed Pearson in the techniques of hand waving and hand shaking, in the art of political conversation, and in the conservation of energy. When their car passed the riding boundary, Farquhar told the new candidate, "You can stop waving now, we're out of the constituency."

OPPOSITE
The Prime Minister and Mrs. Pearson as Canada will remember them: a striking portrait by Ashley & Crippen, of Toronto. *Miller Services Limited.*

In the by-election on October 25, 1948, Pearson received a plurality of 1236 votes, nine less than Farquhar in 1945. On January 26, 1949, Louis St. Laurent and C. D. Howe escorted the new Member of Parliament into the House of Commons for the first time.

It was not a bad time to become a politician, particularly on the government side. Depression had not followed war, as in 1919. Although there were strains on the economy, almost full employment was maintained as the armed forces were demobilized and returned to civilian employment. A boom and inflation, rather than depression and deflation, characterized this post-war period.

The government was determined that at the least the horrors of the thirties would not recur. The transition to the peace-time economy was carefully prepared, within the framework of private enterprise. Government factories were sold off, private companies were given favourable terms, investment was encouraged. Inevitably at a time of inflation, strikes took place and industrial relations for a while looked bilious, as workers tried to catch up after years of war-time control, and depression before that. Nevertheless, the signs of prosperity and abundant employment were everywhere, and for several years unemployment remained at a negligible figure.

Strikes were only one sign of a general determination to exploit the new-found security and prosperity. The economic side of life, though of primary importance, was not the only preoccupation of the period. The government had studied the experience of the First World War, and had made very substantial provision for veterans of the armed forces. A large sum of money was set aside to allow veterans to continue their education, and for the first time thousands of young men and women attended college through their veterans' scholarships. The colleges, which had been denuded of male students during the war, were given emergency aid to help them absorb the flood.

Canada had never had a very high proportion of university graduates, when compared with the United States. There had always been enough, but the demand, outside the professions and the civil service, had never been very great. South of the border, great state educational systems had provided what some people regarded as the birthright of the citizen. These systems had been studied, and to some extent imitated in Canada, especially in the west, but the results had lagged behind the Americans'. After 1945 and the influx of veterans, pressure on the colleges to admit more and more students

54

became irresistible, in spite of lamentations from more conservative academics that mass universities were a contradiction in terms.

The ensuing growth in higher education demanded more money. Where before the war many universities could be more or less self-supporting, afterwards they had no hope of remaining financially independent. Some of the necessary funds, it was hoped, would come from the federal government.

In 1949, St. Laurent was persuaded to establish a Royal Commission to look into the state of the arts, letters, and sciences in Canada. Vincent Massey, at loose ends after returning from London, was appointed chairman. Massey could have wished for nothing more, and soon he and his fellow commissioners were hard at work on a report calling for more support for Canadian culture, which they presented to the government in 1951. Two of the recommendations of the report were especially noteworthy: federal aid to universities (which had been previously fenced off behind provincial jurisdiction over education) on the grounds that university education was a national resource; and the creation of a national council to aid the arts through judicious grants to the deserving, be they individuals or institutions.

The federal government acted quickly to give aid to the universities. Prime Minister St. Laurent announced, and finance minister Abbott implemented, a system of per capita grants to all Canadian universities. The vines on the walls of academe were henceforth rooted in more luxuriant soil. The first fruits were sweet and pleasant, but the indirect consequences, the integration of universities into a long list of governmental expenditures and priorities, were less so.

The federal government justified its intervention into provincial fields by referring to the unequal opportunities available to Canadians in different localities across the country. It was acting to provide a common standard, in keeping with its belief that the Canadian nationality demanded a roughly common and equal treatment. Since Canada was one country, regional differences, where they were not merely quaint, should be discouraged. Canadian nationalism was riding high, and provincial identities were, for the moment, correspondingly low.

Culture was only one means for bringing people together. From an engineering standpoint, the problem was one of transportation and communications. In 1945 it was extremely difficult to drive from one end of the country to the other, and the temptation was to detour through the United States.

Except in the central provinces, a picnic or a vacation trip was a major undertaking which only the brave should endure. After 1945, the provincial governments began to bestir themselves. Ontario had already completed, in 1939, Canada's first four-lane highway, the Queen Elizabeth Way, and during the war, construction had proceeded fitfully on a four-lane road from Toronto to Oshawa, the ancestor of the future Highway 401. After the war, construction speeded up.

Here too the federal government decided to intervene. In 1950 finance minister Abbott announced to the assembled provincial representatives that the federal government stood ready to provide matching grants for a Trans-Canada Highway, to be built up to federal standards. Some provinces were understandably reluctant to alter their spending plans to make room for this expenditure too, and there were some provinces which could afford the expense less than others. Premier Duplessis of Quebec stood firm against this federal invasion of provincial jurisdiction, but all, except Duplessis, eventually took the money and built the roads. Even Quebec, after 1960, decided to participate when it discovered that it could save money by doing so. On November 27, 1965, at 11 a.m., premier Joey Smallwood of Newfoundland opened the last stretch of highway, and, incidentally, the first road across Newfoundland. It was just over eighty years since the completion of Canada's first transcontinental railway.

3
Off to the
Cold Wars

PEARSON'S MOVE from undersecretary to Secretary of State for External Affairs was physically easy — down the hall in the East Block of the Parliament Buildings to a corner office overlooking the Peace Tower, the Rideau Club and the American Embassy. The administrative and political climate remained the same. The same people made policy, the same galaxy of diplomatic stars decorated the department and its embassies, and, naturally, the policies were constant.

The basic Canadian policies for the post-war period were the products of circumstance: the decline in British power,

Leaders of the Canadian delegation to the meeting of the North Atlantic Council held in Paris in 1953: Pearson with Brooke Claxton (left), Minister of Defence, and Arnold Heeney, Canada's Permament Representative to the Council.
Public Archives Canada, C-70449.

the expansion of the Soviet Union and the overwhelming economic strength of the United States.

The decline of Britain as a world power was the single greatest change that Canadians had to face. It was more real than apparent. In 1945 Britain still commanded great fleets, administered vast colonies and participated as an equal in "Big Three" conferences with the Soviet Union and the USA. Great ideas and innovative policies still originated in Britain, and British social policies still set the fashions for Canadian intellectuals and political radicals. Even the defeat of Winston Churchill's Conservatives in the British general elections of 1945 was significant for Canadians. Perhaps Canada too, like Britain, would acquire a socialist government in the fullness of time.

For the older generation, Britain was the centre of the world. Mackenzie King, who had spent a generation playing constitutional charades with the British Empire, now worried that the British were declining too quickly and too far. B. K. Sandwell, dean of Canadian journalists, proclaimed in his magazine *Saturday Night* that "any world in which Great Britain has ceased to be an important factor is a world in which Canada, as a distinct political entity, will have ceased to be an important factor also." Sandwell knew that the British economy was weakening, and that British strength was ebbing; like it or not, Canada would have to stand alone in the post-war world.

King's generation, like Sandwell's, was passing from the Canadian scene. It was a younger generation that confronted the Canadian riddle of maintaining a distinct political identity. Before 1945, the task had been simplified by the absence of any serious overseas threat. After 1945 there was communism, the Soviet Union, and the atomic bomb. Canada's "fire-proof house" needed the services of a fire-brigade and Canadians could not afford to bear the burden alone.

Canada's third problem, the United States, was in the eyes of many not a problem at all, but a solution. The very similarity of the United States made identification easy. Americans drove the same cars, went to the same movies, used the same detergents, manufactured most of the soap operas that Canadians listened to on the radio, wrote the hit songs and shared the same problems. They were, however, richer. Canadians, naturally, were both envious and imitative. Some, though a few, deplored the American influence which they equated with vulgarity; American culture was "low-brow," to use the current, convenient American term.

A close association with the United States was a risk and an opportunity that post-war Canada had to take. In an unfamiliar and fearful world the Americans were friendly and reassuring — the one rock of stability in a tide of disintegration. The first choice of the Canadian government was necessarily for stability and security. The preservation of the essential differences between Canada and the United States, though it was never forgotten, had for the moment to take second place.

Security was not intended to be Canada's first post-war priority. Mackenzie King and his cabinet, like most of their countrymen, believed that Canada's main problems would be economic — economic security for the individual, expansion of international trade for the country. King and his colleagues received a rude shock when, on September 6, 1945, word was brought to the Prime Minister that a cypher clerk from the Soviet Embassy was trying to place himself under Canadian protection. The clerk, Igor Gouzenko, had left the embassy with a pile of secret documents which proved the existence of a Soviet spy ring in Canada.

The main object of Soviet espionage was the secret of the atomic bomb. Canada had supplied some uranium to Anglo-American researchers working on the atomic bomb, and the British and Canadians had collaborated in atomic research during the war in a laboratory in the University of Montreal. In 1945 the new atomic centre at Chalk River, up the Ottawa

Pearson attended many Commonwealth Conferences as Canada's chief delegate. The "new" Commonwealth itself, in which India, although a republic, continued to be a member, came into existence in London in 1949. Here Pearson is shown (far left) at the succeeding 1950 conference in Colombo, which sponsored the "Colombo Plan" for cooperative economic development in south and southeast Asia.
Public Archives Canada, C-90455.

fashion fame

Capucci — Velvet lined with chiffon and pleated. The full and slim silhouettes combined in straight-line dress and luxurious evening coat. Buttoned cutaway front.

Antonelli — Yards of velvet . . . mink trimmed, over draped silk. Full blown sleeves—tightly cuffed.

Battilochi — Asymmetric line achieved by contrasting detachable scarf. Natural contours.

Fabiani — Bulky wool. Sailor collar. Wide dolman sleeves. Fullness falls to the back from natural unpadded shoulders.

Carosa — Morning Glory silhouette. High collarless neckline. Fullness below hipline.

Antonelli — Asymmetric neckline. Slender satin. With tiers of side drapery.

Prominent European designers use wool, velvet, satin and mink in these *haute couture* fashions from the pages of *Chatelaine* magazine in October of 1952. Not everyone could afford such elegance, but high fashion reached a level of general interest in the fifties. This interest declined in the "hippie" days of the sixties only to be revived several years later. *Metropolitan Toronto Library Board.*

River from the capital, was just getting under way. For possibly the first time in Canada's experience, the country had a secret that was worth stealing.

Gouzenko's revelations proved to be accurate, and King was horrified. An investigation began; a Royal Commission followed; Canadians were arrested in the dead of night and held incommunicado; trials and convictions proceeded. Even a Member of Parliament, Fred Rose, a communist, was among those convicted. Although there were protests from civil libertarians about the stringent methods adopted, there could be little doubt of the gravity of the situation that had occasioned them.

The discovery of the Soviet spy ring seriously raised the possibility that the war against Naziism had been won only to be replaced by the possibility of war with the Soviet Union. Differences between the western powers and the Russians had been swept under the rug for the duration of the war. Canadian propagandists had pretended that Canadian and Soviet institutions were not far apart after all, and the Canadian Communist (Labour-Progressive) Party loudly supported both the war and the government. Now, however, Canadians remembered that communism was supposed to be a universal philosophy, that world revolution was at least the ultimate goal of Soviet policy, and that Russian society did have certain undesirable features. When the Red Army moved west in the last stages of the war, it brought in its wake Stalin's secret police.

Some Canadians were evidently lost in admiration for the vision of the classless society. This was not Pearson's view, nor was it a belief widely shared in the Canadian diplomatic service. From Moscow the Canadian ambassador reported that Soviet society was in fact highly stratified, and that a new class with well-defined privileges had grown up. In Paris, Mackenzie King was distressed to find the peace conference a forum for the exchange of insults between the Russians and Americans. At the United Nations, genuine exchange of views gave way to public posturing for the galleries and the press at home. In Eastern Europe, communist governments were gradually imposed on most of Russia's neighbours. Finally, in February 1948, Czechoslovakia, the only remaining democracy in the Soviet sphere of influence, succumbed to a communist coup d'état.

Alarm spread throughout Western Europe. The United States had virtually disbanded its ground forces after the end of the war; the British had grave economic problems; the

A dramatic moment recorded in an undramatic way: this photograph of a blackboard was the only photograph taken when the NRX atomic reactor went into operation at Canada's atomic research station, at Chalk River. The time was "0613 hours, July 22" in 1947.
Atomic Energy of Canada Limited.

French and Italians were wracked by internal strife. The only effective army in Europe was the Red Army, and that army's bases were just across the Elbe, in the Russian zone of occupation in Germany. A sudden Russian attack was not hard to imagine, especially in conjunction with internal disturbances by native communists in the western countries.

Canadian missions in London, Washington and Moscow reported on the developing confrontation between the western powers, especially the United States, and the Soviet bloc. While still ambassador in Washington, Pearson analyzed Soviet policy for his government in terms of Soviet security needs — not simply the security of the Soviet Union against outside aggression, but the internal security of the communist leadership. These security concerns, Pearson argued, required a Soviet cordon sanitaire around the Russian homeland. The boundaries of Russian influence would be projected as far out

64

as possible, through the use of threats and bluff, but it was not likely that the Soviet leadership would actually resort to war in order to achieve their ends. The proper response to bluff, in Pearson's opinion, was firmness. If the United Nations would not work to preserve the peace and liberties of its members, then it would have to be replaced by some other organization that excluded the Soviet Union.

This was not a unique point of view in its time, although it was more specific than other contemporary analyses in suggesting a new security organization as a partial solution. The concern for Western Europe was more generalized, and formed an important part of Canada's first major post-war policy statement. Speaking in the Gray Lecture in the University of Toronto's Convocation Hall, St. Laurent told his audience that the Canadian government recognized that "a threat to the liberty of Western Europe" was "a threat to our own way of life." Throughout 1947 St. Laurent amplified this statement of principles. Finally, in September 1947, he delivered a speech drafted by Pearson calling for "an association of democratic and peace-living states willing to accept more specific international obligations in return for a greater measure of national security."

In Western Europe, the British and French had already signed a defensive alliance. After the communist seizure of

The scene at Chalk River in December 1957 when the NRU atomic reactor, a more powerful version of the NRX, went into operation. Atomic Energy of Canada, Ltd., a Crown corporation, had been formed in 1952 to take over operation of the Chalk River research station. *Atomic Energy of Canada Limited.*

power in Czechoslovakia, Britain, France, Belgium, the Netherlands and Luxembourg signed a further alliance, the Brussels Pact. The Canadian government assured them of its sympathy and, more practically, agreed to a British request to participate in secret discussions with the United States on "an Atlantic Security System."

These discussions took place in Washington between March 22 and April 1, 1948. Pearson and Hume Wrong, who was now the Canadian Ambassador in Washington, were the leading members of the Canadian delegation. The three countries, Canada, Britain and the United States, agreed "that a *treaty* should be accomplished and as soon as possible." The treaty would be a "North Atlantic Defence Agreement," and would include Canada, the United States, and the Western European powers.

From an early moment in these negotiations Pearson had two objectives in mind. First, of course, he wanted a security agreement which would encourage the Western Europeans to stand up to the Soviet Union. But he also wanted the security agreement to contain some other, more permanent features. In talks in Washington on July 7, Pearson emphasized that the "North Atlantic defense arrangements" should not be "tied too closely to Soviet intentions. This might mean," he continued, "that if the danger were removed, or appeared to be removed, this justification for a collective system would disappear." A future North Atlantic security organization ought to "have a positive, not merely a negative purpose." Security against communism, in Pearson's mind, should be security of the spirit as well as of the gun. This opinion was shared by the chief American negotiator, Pearson's opposite number, Robert Lovett, and it was embodied in the draft of the North Atlantic Treaty.

In the NATO negotiations, the close relations between the Canadian delegation, Pearson and Wrong and their subordinates, and their American and British counterparts, stood them in good stead. Canada was regarded as one of the major contributors to any future defence agreement, and Canada's representatives were praised for their diplomatic skill. Although not a power of the first rank, Canada was nonetheless a considerable military and economic force. As the French put it, "in view of the role played by Canada in the late war . . . it is justifiable and desirable that it also be included," in discussions between the British, French and Americans. Such consideration fed Canadians' self-esteem. Perhaps the task of

OPPOSITE
1951 found Canadian troops in unfamiliar surroundings: the hills and paddy fields of Korea. *Public Archives Canada, PA-110828.*

67

remaining a "distinct political entity" would not be so difficult after all.

Canada's prominence in the North Atlantic negotiations was tempered by a dispute that arose shortly before the actual signing of the treaty. In the treaty, the second article had been inserted largely on Canada's insistence. This article provided for nonmilitary co-operation among the signatories. The Europeans had accepted this article without notable enthusiasm, and even the British were lukewarm. It had been Pearson and the American negotiator Bob Lovett who had supported the idea. When American enthusiasm waned because of prospective difficulties in Congress, and the new American Secretary of State, Dean Acheson, suggested dropping the article, Pearson and Wrong were left virtually alone in defending their social and economic child. Eventually they prevailed, and a modified promise "to bring about a better understanding of the principles which form the basis of their common civilization" and to co-operate economically was signed by the countries of North America and Western Europe. As the diplomats signed, the United States Marine Corps Band played "I've got plenty of nothin' " and "It ain't necessarily so" from Gershwin's *Porgy and Bess*.

The difficulties over article 2 demonstrated the problems that Canada faced in its diplomacy. As a member of a team, Canada could participate in common enterprises and expect common rewards. But when Canada's opinion or position was an isolated one, it had to bring all its diplomatic forces to bear to secure the inclusion of a watered-down promise to co-operate on unspecific items at an unspecified future time. As Acheson later wryly commented, "Pearson has continually urged the [North Atlantic] Council to set up committees of 'wise men' to find a use for it, which the 'wise men' continually failed to do."

Article 2 also underlined some of the difficulties that Canada faced in its relations with the United States. The Americans were primarily interested in military security. Dean Acheson, as Secretary of State and afterwards, had little patience with "woolly morality in politics," as he described some Canadian foreign policy pronouncements. (Where Pearson had been the son of a Methodist clergyman, Acheson was the son of an Anglican minister from Toronto.) American impatience with certain varieties of Canadian advice created problems for Canadian diplomats, but also highlighted a divergence between the foreign policies of the two countries. As Hume Wrong put it early in 1947,

the consciousness of the people of the United States of their
responsibilities in the world community depends too greatly
on their fear and dislike of the Soviet Union and the communist ideology. This dislike and fear results in distortions
and exaggerations which increase the difficulty of achieving
a negotiated settlement between the US and the USSR.

Pearson with Bulganin
and Khrushchev in 1955.
Public Archives Canada,
C-90373.

As Wrong implied, it also increased the difficulty of securing
harmony of views between Canada and the United States.

The occasional lack of harmony within a broader field of
agreement was to be best illustrated the following year. On
June 25, 1950, the forces of North Korea crossed the 38th
parallel and invaded South Korea. Within a short time they
had achieved an overwhelming military victory. The 25th
of June was a Sunday. Parliament was about to recess for the
summer, and official Ottawa was winding down in anticipation. Pearson and most of his responsible officials, as well as
the Prime Minister, were in their summer cottages. Since Pearson had no phone, the North Korean invasion was already

twenty-six hours old before he got the news that it had taken place. Pearson phoned St. Laurent, and the two men agreed that a unilateral American response to the invasion was undesirable, since it involved the risk of a general war. In fact, Pearson believed the Americans would do little, and was surprised to learn that president Truman had decided to send aid to the South Koreans. At the same time, the American government resolved to act within the United Nations organization to preserve peace.

The American decision to use the United Nations was

Pearson with Churchill during the latter's visit to Ottawa, in 1952. *Public Archives Canada, C-90369.*

received with satisfaction in Ottawa. Henceforth there would be an institutionalized means of "riding herd" on American policy. American decisions would no longer be unilateral, but subject to multilateral discussion and possible compromise. These reservations on the future were not disclosed to the public which, in any case, was not disposed to hear them. On Korea, Canadian public opinion vociferously supported a policy of action, and there was a widespread expectation that Canada would send help to the Koreans and the Americans. The government obliged, sending first ships and transport planes, and then a volunteer brigade of infantry.

Between 1951 and 1953 Canadian infantry fought as part of a Commonwealth Division in the hills and rice-paddies of Korea. The war of manoeuvre was virtually over, and soon after the Canadians' arrival negotiations began for a cease-fire. These negotiations gave a new meaning to the concept of eternity as United Nations and communist negotiators traded abuse across a conference table. Finally, on July 27, 1953, the cease-fire was signed and the fighting was over. 1557 Canadians were casualties and 312 had died.

Pearson, C. D. Howe and Foster Dulles at a meeting of the Joint US-Canadian Committee on Trade and Economic Affairs in 1954. *Public Archives Canada*, C-20021.

Back in Ottawa another war was being waged on the diplomatic front. By 1951 the Canadian government was engaged in seeking a negotiated peace in Korea, based roughly on the status quo. Its efforts were supported, in varying degrees, by other members of the United Nations. The most reluctant parties were the countries that were doing most of the actual fighting: the Americans, the Koreans (both sides), and the Chinese. Inevitably, differing American and Canadian views of the tactics to be pursued at the United Nations and at the negotiating table caused acrimony between the two allies, and particularly between Acheson and Pearson. The Canadians were fearful of an all-out American decision for war in the Far East, which they regarded as a potentially unmitigated disaster. The Truman administration, however, did not contemplate going further than Korea. An unlimited land war in Asia was not to Truman's, or Acheson's, taste.

The war had another, unexpected, side-effect. The invasion of Korea profoundly disturbed western defence planners, who were uncertain whether it marked the first stage of a world-wide communist attack. Accordingly, it was decided to reinforce western defences in Europe as well as Asia. A brigade group was assembled and sent to Europe in the summer of 1951. As a result of these increased responsibilities the Canadian army more than doubled in size between 1950 and 1951. Canada also undertook to train NATO airmen in Canada, and in 1951 elements of an air division began arriving in Europe. The RCAF was eventually stationed in eastern France, and the army brigade in Germany. Although Canadian troops eventually returned from Korea in 1955, the NATO brigade and air division remained in Europe.

The end of the Korean war found Canada in the throes of an election campaign. St. Laurent and the Liberals soon discovered that the campaign was less of a contest than a pageant. The government was triumphantly returned, and Pearson himself increased his margin over his nearest opponent. While Canada's politics remained stable, other countries changed their governments. In Britain, Winston Churchill and the Conservatives returned to power in 1951. The next year the United States elected Dwight D. Eisenhower and the Republicans to power in Washington. Pearson's friendly rival Acheson was out of office, and John Foster Dulles succeeded him as Secretary of State. Finally, in March 1953, the Russian dictator Stalin died, presumably but not certainly of natural causes. With him died the most ferocious features of his system, and within a few years it was possible for his successor, as General

A moment of frustration at the UN in 1950. *Public Archives Canada, C-90378.*

Pearson, in his capacity as President of the General Assembly, opening the meeting of the UN Steering Committee in October 1952. *United Nations.*

Secretary of the Soviet Communist party, Nikita Khrushchev, to denounce Stalin's crimes and excesses before a party congress.

These changes suggested the possibility of a change in international alignments, and Pearson was anxious to find out what might now be possible. At the invitation of Soviet foreign minister Molotov, he visited the Soviet Union in October 1955, along with Mitchell Sharp of the department of Trade and Commerce, and George Ignatieff and John Holmes of External Affairs. Press coverage was provided by, among others, René Lévesque, a young reporter from the CBC's French network. Sharp's mission was immediately productive: a Canadian-Russian trade agreement was signed, much to the relief and pleasure of St. Laurent and Howe, back in Ottawa. The diplomats had a more generalized brief as they were to cover the Soviets' political landscape and investigate Russian feelings about NATO and the problem of Western European security. As might have been expected, the Russian leaders vigorously condemned NATO and denied that there was any problem with respect to the security of Western Europe. The foreign policy goal of the USSR, they stated, was "peaceful co-

In November 1952, while Pearson was President of the General Assembly, President-elect Eisenhower visited the UN in New York. Here he is being greeted by Pearson, while Foster Dulles, soon to become US Secretary of State, and Trygve Lie, UN Secretary-General, look on.
United Nations.

OVERLEAF
Pearson delivering his opening statement as President of the United Nations General Assembly in February 1953. Trygve Lie, Secretary-General, is on his right, and Andrew Cordier, Lie's Executive Assistant, is on his left.
United Nations.

existence," i.e., peaceful competition between capitalism and communism, always bearing in mind that communism would inevitably win out. Drinks followed talk. It became apparent that Pearson and his companions were expected to join in a drinking competition for the honour of Canada and capitalism. When, hours later, the Canadian party staggered out, they did so "straightly, heads up, with fixed determination and without any assistance." To their great satisfaction, Bulganin and Khrushchev were "in worse condition than we were," as Pearson happily recorded.

The gulf between east and west might not be as wide as reported. Pearson had no desire to change the direction of Canadian policy, but he hoped to take a more consistently moderate and less rhetorically extravagant line than the Americans — no difficult task when the American Secretary of State was John Foster Dulles. Dulles' rigid anti-communism and his public moralizing on good and evil in international behaviour contrasted with Pearson's softer public approach. In 1955 the two men publicly disagreed on the proper policy to follow in a dispute between Nationalist China (restricted to one large offshore island, Taiwan or Formosa, and several smaller ones) and the communist Chinese. And when the Canadian delegation at the United Nations proposed a compromise designed to let in new members previously excluded by the great powers' mutual vetoes, Dulles was incensed. After a sulphurous exchange with Canadian diplomats in Washington, however, the Secretary calmed down.

The Canadian compromise of 1955, which was negotiated by a delegation headed by Pearson's colleague Paul Martin, had a profound impact on the United Nations. The membership was noticeably expanded, and the old Latin-American-European axis which had ruled the roost began to lose control to a newer "third world" grouping which was less than automatically pro-western or pro-American. The Canadian government had anticipated this development, fully realizing that western and Canadian interests might not be as kindly treated thereafter, but judging that an unrepresentative United Nations would be the worse of the two alternatives.

Thus when a new diplomatic crisis arose, in 1956, the United Nations was a very different body from the one that had gone to war in Korea. The issues were different too. This time it was not communist aggression, but an attack led by three of Canada's friends, Britain, France and Israel, on a country for which most Canadians felt no identity and little sympathy, Egypt.

Pearson knew virtually every statesman of international stature. Here he is greeting Dean Acheson, then US Secretary of State, and Anthony Eden, Britain's Foreign Secretary. *United Nations.*

The origin of the Suez crisis of 1956 lay in the growing weakness of Great Britain. By 1955 most of the British colonial empire in Asia had disappeared, and most of what was left was scheduled for independence in the foreseeable future. In Africa the British were also slowly divesting themselves of responsibility for their vast colonial territories. Under these circumstances the British government, now led by Anthony Eden, decided to wind up the British military occupation of the Suez Canal Zone, and to hand over the canal and the surrounding territory to the Egyptian government of Colonel Gamal Abdel Nasser, in 1955.

The next year, 1956, the British and American governments suddenly withdrew from an agreement to lend money to Egypt for Nasser's prize development project, the Aswan High Dam across the Nile. Nasser, in revenge, nationalized the Suez Canal Company, which was still a private but largely British-owned corporation. Eden saw this as a personal betrayal. He decided that the "Hitler of the Nile" would have to be taught a lesson, and in alliance with the French and the Israelis, the British began to plan the invasion of Egypt.

This invasion, if carried to a conclusion, would inevitably involve the rest of the British Commonwealth, whether or not the other members favoured the project. The old empire had been slowly and painfully converted into a Commonwealth of free nations. It was no longer a tiny club consisting of Britain and the white dominions, but a multi-racial grouping of widely divergent states, a miniature English-speaking version of the United Nations. The Canadian government accepted the change and attached some importance to the new Commonwealth as a lowest common denominator of common interest among states that might otherwise move in different, perhaps opposite, directions. Of these states, the Canadian government professed a particularly high regard for India. India, as everyone knew, would certainly oppose any attempt at the re-establishment of British colonialism in any former imperial territory.

Pearson himself took a jaundiced view of any British attempt to turn nostalgia into foreign policy. It was not that Pearson's relations with the British were bad, as his friendships in the United Kingdom stretched back forty years. But the Canadians were well-acquainted with Britain's economic problems as these had emerged after the Second World War, and they seriously doubted that Britain could afford to play at being a great power any longer.

The eruption of the Suez Canal crisis seemed to demonstrate the truth of the Canadian perception of British weakness. On August 6, 1956, Pearson wrote to his friend Norman Robertson, the Canadian High Commissioner in London, that in his view a British attempt to use force against Egypt would "split the Commonwealth" and possibly precipitate a rift between Britain and the United States. As an additional embarrassing complication, Egypt could appeal to the United Nations for help against the British aggressor, and the United Nations would presumably heed the call. Accordingly, Pearson instructed Robertson to make "every possible effort to prevent a chain of developments which would result in Anglo-French military force being exerted against Egypt in a way which would split the Commonwealth, weaken the Anglo-American alliance, and have general consequences which would benefit nobody but Moscow."

Despite the advice from Canada, the British decided to go ahead and recover the Canal, peacefully if possible, but if necessary, by force. A plan was worked out with the French, and Israel's co-operation was secured. On October 29 the Israelis began the invasion of Egypt. A pre-arranged Anglo-French ultimatum was handed to both sides, demanding an immediate cease-fire. Israel, as expected, accepted the ultimatum, while Egypt did not. The British began bombing Egyptian airfields and this was followed a few days later by the landing of British and French troops.

Although Canada had proffered advice at earlier stages, it was not informed of the British plans until after the fact. The British saw no point in telling the Canadians what they intended to do, since Canadian disapproval was certain. Disapproval was the mildest reaction. Prime Minister St. Laurent was outraged. In public he made a scathing reference to "the supermen of Europe," and in private, he was even more forceful. Canadian public opinion was sharply divided. A Gallup Poll reported 43% in favour of the Anglo-French action, 40% opposed, and 17% with no opinion. In a famous comment, a British magazine described Canadian reaction as "almost tearful . . . like finding a beloved uncle arrested for rape."

Once the British bombing was underway, St. Laurent received a letter from Eden justifying his action and asking for support. Pearson and his officials helped St. Laurent draft his reply, deploring the impact of the British invasion on the United Nations, the Commonwealth, and Anglo-American relations. The last was the worst. "It is hard," he wrote, "for a Canadian to think of any consideration — other than national survival or safety — as more important." In Pearson's view, the British had misjudged every aspect of their invasion of Egypt, including the likelihood of military success. In the event, this too was denied them. American reaction was hostile; India was loud in condemnation; the unity of the Commonwealth was imperilled; the British pound and French franc teetered. The British had no option but to draw back, discredited, from this miscalculated operation. As in the thirties, the execution and conception of British policy were shown in the worst possible light. Pearson later commented that "it is a sad reflection on the judgment of those responsible that only now are they beginning to realize the fact that failure was likely from the outset and that the consequences of failure, economically and politically, would be heavy and hard to bear."

Brooding on the British failure and the world's reaction thereto, Pearson flew to New York to attend the emergency debates of the United Nations. The Suez question was already before the Security Council, and there was considerable danger not only of United Nations condemnation of the Anglo-French action, but a far-reaching disruption of western diplomatic relationships if the crisis continued. Pearson, to paraphrase Sir John A. Macdonald many years before, was going to "get Eden and Company out of the hole into which their own imbecility had plunged them." In discussions with the cabinet before his departure, Pearson had mentioned the possibility of interposing a United Nations emergency police force between the combatants. This would bring stability to the fighting zone, and would satisfy one of the ostensible excuses for Anglo-French intervention. Behind the physical and symbolic screen of this police force, the British, French and Israelis could withdraw with some vestige of dignity. St. Laurent agreed to support the idea.

When Pearson arrived in New York, he found resolutions demanding a cease-fire and withdrawal already sailing through the General Assembly. Britain, France and a forlorn band of their allies voted impotently against these resolutions, which were carried overwhelmingly. As far as Pearson was concerned, withdrawal was not enough. Something had to be inserted into the situation or the world would be back where it had all started, just before the invasion. By persistent lobbying among other delegations, Pearson and his officials insinuated the idea that now was the time for a United Nations police force.

On November 3, Pearson moved a Canadian resolution asking the Secretary General of the United Nations, Dag Hammarskjold, to "submit . . . a plan for the setting up, with the consent of the nations concerned, of an emergency international United Nations force to secure and supervise the cessation of hostilities" in accordance with a previous cease-fire

The formal opening of the St. Lawrence Seaway in June 1959 by Her Majesty the Queen and President Eisenhower. The project was launched by the St. Laurent Government, but Diefenbaker (behind the Queen) was Prime Minister when it was completed.
The Seaway. Public Archives Canada.

resolution. Pearson's resolution passed, 57 for, 0 against, with 19 abstentions. Canada immediately offered troops to the proposed force, and by November 7 enough countries had followed suit to make the United Nations Emergency Force (UNEF) feasible. Under the cloak of United Nations action the British and French withdrew their troops, with the British proclaiming that their invasion had in fact paved the way for this desirable result.

The next problem was persuading the other combatants to accept the force. Hammarskjold approached Egypt, which reluctantly agreed. President Nasser imposed two significant conditions: the force, he declared, should be obliged to leave Egypt at Egypt's demand; and Canada, an associate of Britain, must not furnish troops to UNEF. For Pearson and his Liberal colleagues it was unthinkable that after Canada's strenuous and prominent role in getting the United Nations to establish a peace force, Canada should not be allowed to provide any of the troops, especially after publicly offering them. Canadian public opinion would not easily forgive such a gratuitous slight. The government was already facing fierce criticism from traditionally-minded Conservatives and hardly deserved the additional political burden of Egyptian ingratitude. Frantic telegrams passed between Ottawa, New York and Cairo. Eventually, the Egyptians reluctantly accepted Canadian troops, but not the Queen's Own Rifles, who had been originally assigned to Middle East duty. "What we needed," Pearson afterwards wrote, "was the East Kootenay Anti-Imperialistic Rifles!" The Israelis also agreed to withdraw from the Sinai desert back to their own borders, but only on condition that the United Nations guarantee free passage for shipping up the Gulf of Aqaba, between Egyptian Sinai and Saudi Arabia, to Israel's southern port of Eilat. UN troops accordingly took up positions along the shores of the strategic gulf.

Naturally, Pearson believed that he and Canada could take credit for a job well done. Canada's immediate diplomatic objectives had been secured. The division in the Commonwealth had been minimized, although the scar of memory remained. The Anglo-American alliance survived more or less intact, and a total, formal humiliation of the British at the United Nations had been averted. For these blessings, Pearson later recorded, the British were "grateful." Nevertheless, the Suez affair had done incalculable damage to the complicated structure of international friendship on which Canada relied, and the mere preservation of appearances was a trivial compensation. The British ships sailing away from the Suez Canal carried with them a cargo of national despondency, if not a feeling of national disgrace. A reduced Great Britain survived the disaster, but the British Empire did not.

One of Pearson's most valuable assistants during the strenuous days of the crisis was the Canadian ambassador in Egypt, Herbert Norman. Norman was a distinguished diplomat of long standing. He was also haunted by an allegation that twenty years before, as a graduate student at Harvard, he had attended a marxist study group. In a fearful, militantly anti-communist United States, this was enough to damn him. Pearson had investigated the charges, found them baseless, and exonerated Norman. When they were revived before an irresponsible American Senate committee, it was too much. Norman committed suicide.

Most Canadians were unimpressed by the hunt for hidden communists in the United States after the Second World War. Many of the charges were unfounded, and even where apparently proven, were largely trivial. The cure of witch-hunting seemed to be worse than the malady of communism. Now it seemed that this curse was spreading into Canada and victimizing innocent Canadians. When Norman's death was announced to a shocked House of Commons, the reaction was severe. "God," a Canadian reporter muttered to himself (to be overheard by an American), "I hate Americans."

Pearson was grieved by the loss of a trusted colleague. He regarded the causes of the loss as intolerable. A stiff note was sent to Washington demanding that the executive branch of the American government cease transmitting Canadian security information to a sensation-happy Congress. Otherwise, Canada would review its policy of co-operation on security matters. Eisenhower's government profusely apologized, but it could do little to control the manner in which Congress conducted itself.

As a diplomatic incident, the Norman affair was laid to rest, but as an incident in the broader pattern of Canadian-American relations, it went further. Many Canadians, especially on the Conservative side, resented what they interpreted to be Canadian subservience to the Americans. In November 1956, according to this view, Pearson had sided with the Americans against the British. Now, they thought, the Americans' true nature had displayed itself. If one test of Canada's continued sense of identity is a lively resentment of the United States, the test succeeded in 1956. When the Gallup poll asked Canadians whether they would like to join the United States in that year, only 10% replied in the affirmative, down from 18% in 1950 and 21% in 1943.

In the 1957 general election, which resulted in the defeat of the St. Laurent government, external affairs became an issue for the first time in decades, and Pearson found that his previously uncontroversial conduct of an all-party foreign policy was getting him and the government into trouble. Ultimately it proved impossible to determine how much weight voters gave to foreign policy as an issue in the campaign, but analysts could agree that "some" was a proper conclusion.

Political storms pass. In October 1957 Pearson was sitting in his new basement office in the Centre Block on Parliament Hill waiting for the opening of the new Parliament. As member for Algoma East, his concerns and his quarters were notably less spacious than those he had enjoyed as a minister. When the Canadian Press called and asked for comments, Pearson was puzzled: "On what?" Pearson had not yet heard that he had just been awarded the Nobel Prize for Peace for his United Nations diplomacy the year before. Pearson's comment was worthy of his Methodist upbringing and Ontario heritage: "Gosh!"

For Pearson the otherwise dismal year 1957 reached a happy climax in December when a special SAS flight picked him up in Ottawa for the trip to Scandinavia. On December 11, at Aula University in Norway, he delivered his Nobel laureate's speech. In a characteristically graceful address, he spoke of the tragedy of life in the twentieth century, and of the ironic disparity between man's technical achievements and his lack of progress as a moral being. The fine liberal virtue of tolerance flourished in the individual, but failed at the collective level, especially in the state. To illustrate his point, Pearson recalled for his audience an experience during the Second World War in London.

I was reading in bed, and to drown out or at least to take my mind off the bombs, I reached out and turned on the radio. I was fumbling aimlessly with the dial when the room was flooded with the beauty and peace of Christmas carol music. Glorious waves of it wiped out the sound of war and conjured up visions of happier peace-time Christmases. Then the announcer spoke — in German. For it was a German station and they were Germans who were singing those carols. Nazi bombs screaming through the air with their message of war and death; German music drifting through the air with its message of peace and salvation. When we resolve the paradox of those two sounds from a single national source, we will, at last, be in a good position to understand and solve the problem of peace and war.

4

Prairie Avenger

PEARSON CONDUCTED his external policy against the solid backdrop of a stable Liberal government sustained by a solid majority in the House of Commons. Ultimately, there was no question that the government could get its programs through the House, a task which was facilitated by a comparatively weak and ineffective opposition. St. Laurent presided with dignity and charm over all under the sunny public nickname of "Uncle Louis," sallying forth every fourth year to dispose of the opposition for another term. In 1949 the Liberals had won their biggest majority to date, confounding pessimists who believed that after fourteen years of office, enough was enough. In 1953, the performance was repeated.

Part of the Liberals' election success could be ascribed to the confident and competent direction of the party's election strategists, fuelled with plentiful funds from the business community. For the opposition Conservatives, there was only despair. After their fifth successive defeat, in 1953, one Conservative MP, George Nowlan, asked one of the national organizers, "Dear God, where did we ever get that platform?" The organizer, Dalton Camp, replied, "I professed surprise that he did not know. He was, after all, the party's national president."

In the low ebb of Conservative hopes, there were still some promising eddies. In 1952, the aging Liberal government of New Brunswick was replaced by a Conservative administration. In 1956, Nova Scotia swung into the Conservative column, under Robert Stanfield. Ontario regularly returned Premier Leslie Frost with Conservative majorities. Only in Prince Edward Island, Manitoba, and Newfoundland did the Liberals keep provincial power. In Ottawa, however, things went on as usual.

OPPOSITE
Lester Bowles Pearson in 1963, the year he became Prime Minister.
Public Archives Canada, PA-57932.

87

Yet even there changes were evident. Douglas Abbott, the popular and breezy finance minister, and Brooke Claxton, one of the party's election strategists and the defence minister, both left politics.

St. Laurent, returning home after a round-the-world trip, was distressed to find some of his most active colleagues quitting the cabinet. Worse, the Prime Minister himself was exhausted by his trip, and began to lapse into long fits of depression and, consequently, inaction. But the economy was booming again, after a brief recession, and the opposition had no obvious issues to exploit. In a Gallup poll in April 1956 the Liberals were supported by 45% of the electorate; the Conservatives lagged with 17%, behind the undecided.

St. Laurent's frequent depressions left the party and the cabinet with no pre-eminent leadership. On some issues this was provided by the Minister of Trade and Commerce, the Rt. Hon. C. D. Howe, but Howe was far less than a surrogate Prime Minister. When C. D. wanted to make his opinions count, however, he could push his measures through a reluctant and doubtful cabinet which remained sceptical of the wisdom of his political decisions. In 1955, Howe had suffered a Parliamentary defeat over his defence production act and had become, in the opinion of some ministers, "a political liability."

Shortly after the war large petroleum deposits had been discovered in Alberta, and since 1952 Howe had been considering the feasibility of a pipeline to bring western natural gas to the east. In 1953 he informed the House of Commons that "the only reliable supply of natural gas for the provinces of Ontario and Quebec must be from western Canada by means of an all-Canadian pipeline." Studies and negotiations continued. "I have never started anything I could not finish," Howe wrote. In 1956 his project was ready. The pipeline would be built by private enterprise, with the aid of a short-term government loan. Trans-Canada Pipelines, the chosen agent, was controlled in the United States.

For construction to start in 1956 a bill had to pass through Parliament by the beginning of June. This gave a hostage to fortune. To achieve success, all the opposition had to do was delay passage of the bill until after the deadline, and the opposition could do that, despite the government's majority, by talking the bill out. The only defence against an opposition filibuster was "closure," a majority vote to end debate and force a division. Closure had been introduced by Sir Robert Borden in 1913 to end the interminable debate over a Cana-

OPPOSITE
Ballerina Mary Jago dancing in the Bluebird pas de deux in a National Ballet of Canada production of *The Sleeping Beauty*. Ballet, late to develop in Canada, shared in the great expansion of artistic activity that took place after the Second World War. The Winnipeg Ballet, founded as an amateur effort in 1939, attained full professional status in 1950 and became the Royal Winnipeg Ballet in 1952. The National Ballet of Canada, based in Toronto, was founded in 1951, and the Grands Ballets Canadiens, in Montreal, came into existence in 1957. Grants from the Canada Council have helped these companies to reach international status and to attract the collaboration of international guest stars. They have brought ballet to every important city in Canada and have performed in many centres abroad.
Photo courtesy of The National Ballet of Canada.

Prime Minister St. Laurent
paying his last respects
to Mackenzie King as his
body lay in state in the
Hall of Fame of the
Parliament Buildings
in July 1950.
Public Archives Canada,
C-22234.

dian Navy versus a monetary contribution to Great Britain.
It had last been used by R. B. Bennett in the thirties. The
Liberal cabinet, foreseeing opposition obstruction, decided to
move closure at the beginning of the debate.

This ensured that the subject of the Parliamentary debate
would be closure, not the pipeline. Howe had hoped that his
pipeline would be recognized as a great national project like
the CPR and Trans-Canada Airlines, another of his legislative

children. But it was he who had to move the fateful motion "that further consideration of this resolution shall be the first business of the Committee and shall not further be postponed." The result, Pearson remembered, was "a wild and irrational struggle, a Parliamentary debacle."

Pearson had participated in the cabinet discussions that preceded the introduction of the pipeline bill into Parliament. As debate dragged on, all the government's resources were thrown into the fray. At last, Pearson felt it his duty to speak too, "in the first truly partisan political speech I had made in eight years in the House of Commons." In a slashing attack on the Conservatives, he defended the government's bill and declared that the opposition's issue of American involvement was false. "Let us get ahead and pass this bill," he concluded, "and take one more step in national development." The next night, June 6, the bill was given third and final reading. After speeding through the Senate where, as an historian has noted, "its actual content was more thoroughly debated in a day than it had been during a month in the House," the bill received royal assent on June 7.

Pearson's own position within the Liberal party was enhanced by his speech. With St. Laurent's visible decline, the

George Drew, leader of the Conservative opposition for all but a few months of the St. Laurent ministry.
Public Archives Canada, C-11578.

question of the next leader was emerging again, and Pearson's speech was interpreted by some as an attempt to "catch Walter" – the finance minister, Walter Harris, an obvious leadership contender.

This may have been the only bright spot in the pipeline debate for the Liberals. The party had won the battles of facts and votes, but it had lost, decisively, the battle of illusion. Regardless of the merits of the case, the Liberals had demonstrated the arrogant way in which a large Parliamentary majority could outvote the opposition. The "tyranny of the majority" was a sensitive issue in Canada, and abuse from the minority was more readily tolerated. Now, in the press at least, the opposition had a cause: the rights of Parliament.

The very weakness of the Conservatives was an advantage. Previously, the Conservatives had run as an alternative government against the Liberals under a man who looked like a Prime Minister, George Drew. By competing in the Liberals' league, on the enemy's chosen ground, they helped to ensure their own defeat. But shortly after the pipeline debate, Drew fell ill and resigned as Conservative leader. In his place, the Conservatives selected the MP for Prince Albert, John Diefenbaker.

Diefenbaker looked younger than his sixty-one years. Although he was a senior Member of Parliament, he was hardly one of his party's elder statesmen, since his background and his temperament were far removed from the traditional Tory centre of gravity in Toronto. He was a small-town lawyer who had made his reputation as a defence lawyer in criminal cases and who perceived himself as a perpetual champion of the underdog. Diefenbaker's rhetorical technique provoked scorn from the sophisticated; as they soon learned, he was an exceedingly able public speaker, with a distinctive style, exhortatory, emotional and humorous by turns. He could now turn these qualities on the Liberals.

The Liberals had already decided to keep their leader for another election, despite his failing health. The party would run behind him, one declared, "if we have to run him stuffed." The spring session of Parliament in 1957 was unremarkable. The finance minister, Walter Harris, brought in a surplus and decreed a six-dollar-a-month increase for old age pensioners, from $40 to $46. Harris had resisted a larger sum because of the danger of inflation. He was, in consequence, dubbed "Six-buck Harris," a fatal label. Soon afterwards Parliament was dissolved and an election called for June 10, 1957.

It was a beautiful spring for Diefenbaker, but not for

the Liberals. St. Laurent and his cabinet went to the electorate on their record, promising little except a continuation of sound government. Most commentators expected that they would be re-elected for precisely that reason, citing the proverbial apathy of the Canadian electorate. Underneath the apathy, however, there was an unexpected discontent. "The Canadian people want more," a Conservative adviser wrote. "They ask for vision in their statesmen, a sense of national purpose and national destiny. They are offered prosperity and the welfare state. There is nothing wrong in this but it is not enough. 'Man does not live by bread alone.'" Surfeited by bread, the electorate was bored.

The Liberals found the growing signs of impending defeat hard to believe. Thin crowds, unenthusiastic responses, disastrous mistakes told the story of the Liberal campaign. Meanwhile Diefenbaker steamed about the country, mobilizing opposition with tales of Liberal misdeeds, under the slogan "Time for a change." The Liberals' climactic rally in Toronto was a fiasco, and Pearson left Toronto for Algoma East with a "gloomy foreboding."

On the evening of June 10 the Liberals and the country watched Canada's first televised election returns. The Liberals lost seats everywhere, and cabinet ministers tumbled from Nova Scotia to the prairies. C. D. Howe, Walter Harris and Robert Winters were among the fallen. Diefenbaker's Conservatives held 112 seats, the Liberals 105, the CCF 25, Social Credit 19 and others, 4. St. Laurent decided that his government had been decisively repudiated, and resigned. On June 21 John Diefenbaker became the first Conservative Prime Minister since 1935.

After turning over his department to Diefenbaker, who was temporarily his own Minister of External Affairs, Pearson found himself with nothing to do. His own seat was relatively safe, although he had held it by a reduced margin — no mean feat for an absentee member. With Ottawa in the summer doldrums, he hung around the house and got in the way of domestic order.

This long vacation was interrupted on September 2 by a call to come at once to St. Laurent's summer retreat at St. Patrick, Quebec. With Lionel Chevrier, the former Minister of Transport, he arrived in Quebec City on September 4. En route to St. Patrick, St. Laurent's family explained the reason for the call. St. Laurent had been depressed ever since the election. He knew that he was unequal to carrying on as Liberal leader and leader of the opposition in Parliament, but

he could not bring himself to announce his resignation. The family now asked Pearson and Chevrier to persuade St. Laurent that he would not be betraying his trust if he resigned now. When the three men actually met, St. Laurent indicated that he was agreeable to resigning, provided that his resignation was not interpreted as desertion.

The two younger men gave their leader such comfort as they could. At the suggestion of St. Laurent's son, Pearson drafted a resignation statement, which Chevrier approved. St. Laurent approved in his turn, and the statement was released to the press. "I have never . . . taken part in a more painful task," Pearson wrote in his memoirs.

The question of Liberal party leadership now became acute. A convention was scheduled for January 1958, in Ottawa. Walter Harris was out of the running, Claxton and Abbott were no longer in politics, and only two serious candidates were left: Pearson and Paul Martin, the former Minister of Health and Welfare. Martin was a strong candidate, a successful minister and a prominent and effective campaigner. To the party hierarchy, however, Pearson seemed a better candidate, and a better bet to defeat Diefenbaker. At the convention Pearson defeated Martin by 1084 votes to 305.

C. D. Howe (right) at the ceremony in 1941 marking the joining of the Canadian and American sections of the oil pipeline connecting Portland, Maine, with Montreal. Its construction was a vital wartime measure, as it greatly reduced the distance tankers had to travel through submarine-infested waters. Fifteen years later a greater pipeline project was to end Howe's political career. *Public Archives Canada, C-7485.*

3 + 4 + 1, by Paul-Emile Borduas (1956). Borduas was one of the best-known and most influential of the post-war Canadian painters. His restless, inquiring mind sought freedom from convention and eventually freedom from subject-matter. The coterie that he headed in Montreal were known as the Automatistes, for they believed that an artist should express himself spontaneously, in whatever forms and colours occurred to him. Titles were an afterthought — whatever might be suggested by the canvas that resulted from the automatic process. For years Borduas worked by day and painted at night, with the strange result that he discovered light only late in life. Thereafter, as in this picture, painted four years before his death, large white areas appeared on his canvases and glowing colours, formerly characteristic, disappeared. *The National Gallery of Canada, Ottawa.*

The Liberals were delighted to have a Nobel-prizewinner at their head. Soon, they hoped, he would defeat Diefenbaker in Parliament and at the polls. The tactic was simple. In his first speech as leader of Her Majesty's Loyal Opposition, Pearson was to demand that Diefenbaker's government resign forthwith, as a token of their incapacity and inability to deal with the country's real problems, which only the Liberals understood. The Liberals would then reassume the mantle of government and "implement Liberal policies," as Pearson's non-confidence motion described them.

Pearson's speech dwelt on the growing weakness of the Canadian economy since mid-1957. Time-honoured Liberal policies were prescribed as a cure. Unwittingly, however, Pearson presented Diefenbaker with the chance of a lifetime, "a better opportunity that day than ever subsequently." Some months earlier a reporter, friendly to the Conservatives, had uncovered a secret report from within the Department of Trade and Commerce analyzing the growing weakness of the Canadian economy and predicting a rise in unemployment and a decline in exports during the rest of 1957. The report was dated March 1957. It was "political dynamite." In his reply to Pearson, Diefenbaker lit the fuse and tossed the dynamite at the surprised opposition.

When the smoke cleared, Diefenbaker had demolished Pearson in a brilliant debating speech, dissolved Parliament, and stumped the country denouncing the iniquities and arrogance of the Liberals. Diefenbaker pitched his appeal to his "fellow-Canadians" on the evangelical level. Eyes flashing, voice trumpeting, he summoned them to follow him and his "Vision." "This is the vision, One Canada," Diefenbaker orated. "One Canada where Canadians will have preserved to them the control of their own economic and political destiny. Sir John A. Macdonald saw Canada from east to west: he opened the west. I see a new Canada — a Canada of the North." Pearson had virtually nothing that he could raise against Diefenbaker, whose government was too recent to sport any visible misdeeds. The Liberals tried to stem the tide with the slogan, "Peace, Prosperity, Pearson," but one journalist suggested that a better one would be "Tea and Sympathy."

Pearson got the sympathy, but not the votes. At first he naively believed that he might do well, and advisers who knew better spared his feelings as he went through the dreary routine of a losing campaign. When the results came in, the Liberals were wiped out west of Kenora and the Conservatives had

Lester Pearson, Louis St. Laurent and Paul Martin join hands at the Liberal convention in January 1958 that chose Pearson as the new party leader.
Public Archives Canada, PA-110785. Capital Press.

scored a genuine national landslide. Diefenbaker won 208 seats out of 265 and an absolute majority of the popular vote. The Liberals were left with 49 seats and 33.6% of the vote, their lowest ever totals in both categories. Even Quebec followed John and gave him 50 out of 75 seats. To Mrs. Pearson's horror, however, Pearson kept his own seat and was assured of a term as leader of the opposition.

In fact, Pearson increased his majority (his colleague Jack Pickersgill, in Newfoundland, increased his as well). Paul Martin and Lionel Chevrier also kept their seats, and in December Paul Hellyer, the youngest survivor of the St. Laurent cabinet, returned to Parliament in a by-election. When Jean Lesage, another ex-minister, resigned from Parliament to become Quebec Liberal leader, his seat was lost to the Conservatives.

Facing the Conservative lions (they not only occupied the entire government side of the House of Commons but spread out and practically surrounded the opposition on the opposition side), Pearson relied on the tried and true talents of Martin, Pickersgill, Chevrier and Hellyer. Together they made a surprisingly effective debating team. Martin in particular was never flustered, and on one occasion, when Pearson failed to get the floor, gave Pearson's speech as his own, with Pearson feeding him the notes one after the other. Martin had a considerable reputation for the rotund expression and the interminable period, "never using one simple word when fifty were needed to confuse and frustrate our political foes," Pearson wrote. Pickersgill, who did not hold Diefenbaker in high esteem, punctured Conservative arguments with sarcastic sallies. Chevrier, Pearson's deskmate, helped to keep the Liberal party alive in Quebec.

Debates in the Commons were comforting for personal morale, but it was the situation outside the House which would determine the parties' future. The Conservatives had used the "secret report" as an election gimmick, but its predictions proved as true, and as unfortunate, for them as for the Liberals. Unemployment went up, and stayed up. Economic indicators turned down. Budgetary surpluses disappeared to be replaced with record peace-time deficits. Diefenbaker's "vision" was slow off the mark in combatting disillusionment with the state of the economy.

Abroad the picture was, if possible, worse. There was no great change between the Liberals' foreign policy and that followed by the Conservatives. On one pending issue, an agreement with the United States integrating continental air defence in the North American Air Defence Command (NORAD), the Conservatives simply confirmed what they found waiting for them. Canada's membership in NATO continued, and Canada remained identified with the Western European-American bloc, despite some initial questioning by the new Minister of External Affairs, Sidney Smith. Within that bloc, Canada's position was already changing. Western Europe had recovered from the war and with the economic re-emergence of Germany and the political rehabilitation of France, Canada's relative importance was no longer what it had been. The same factors obtained at the United Nations, where Canada was necessarily dwarfed by more powerful nations, and where the post-war group of middle powers found agreement among themselves more difficult than before. Canada continued to work away, helpfully, constructively, in

disarmament conferences and in the various United Nations emergency forces, but the Canadian contribution was no longer as essential as it had been, and the Canadian presence no longer, perhaps, quite as important.

The first break for the opposition came in 1959. The Diefenbaker government was forced to announce cancellation of the development and production of an advanced Canadian supersonic fighter, the Avro Arrow, or CF-105. The government could not afford the rapidly mounting costs, and the plane was virtually unsaleable. The government had virtually no other choice than to cancel, but the decision was understandably unpopular, both to the skilled workers immediately involved, and to Canadians at large. The cancellation of the Arrow signified a psychological set-back for a people who took pride in Canada's advanced technology; the Arrow was a highly visible symbol of that technology. The electorate expected more, not less, industrial development and Diefenbaker's own "vision" – confident, expansionist – had exploited the popular mood. National pride and nationalism suffered a defeat, and it was a defeat that Diefenbaker himself could not survive.

Discontent with the unfolding of the "vision" grew slowly, and then mostly in eastern, urban areas. In the west, and in rural areas generally, the Conservatives' policies were much more successful and much more popular. Alvin Hamilton not only survived but grew popular in the difficult portfolio of agriculture with a succession of wheat sales and rural redevelopment schemes. George Hees, the Minister of Trade and Commerce, made a splash with spectacular trade promotions and easily withstood opposition battering in the House of Commons. Howard Green commanded affection, if not always respect, for his policies in external affairs. Despite the creditable records of individuals, the Diefenbaker cabinet did not collectively seem impressive.

Every cabinet has its liabilities. There are errors of omission, leaving out the right man in the right place, and of commission, putting the wrong man in the definitely wrong place. Diefenbaker was strongly criticized for omitting talent from his vast range of backbenchers, although it is difficult to imagine, with 208 to choose from, how he could invariably have made the right choice. But even with a margin for error, the Conservative cabinet ministers from Quebec were not impressive.

The Conservatives had done better under Diefenbaker in Quebec than under any leader since Macdonald. Diefen-

OPPOSITE
Pearson's victory salute to the leadership convention.
Public Archives Canada, PA-110786. Capital Press.

baker's fifty seats in that province seemed to prove that Quebec, politically, was swept by the same current of feeling that brought the rest of the country into line behind "the Chief." As usual, beneath the appearance, there lurked a more practical reality, in this case, "le chef," Premier Duplessis. Diefenbaker's own position in Quebec's affections was not strong, and even his concession of simultaneous translation in Parliament, in itself a considerable improvement in the conduct of debate, did not rally much public support. His political position in Quebec therefore depended to a peculiar degree on the calibre of his Quebec cabinet ministers and as time passed it became obvious that this was not strong. One minister was reputed to be unable to understand enough English to follow discussions in cabinet, where he worked on crossword puzzles instead.

The Conservatives' arrival in office had been heralded by a string of provincial election victories. These had continued in 1958 and 1959 with the defeat of the Liberal governments in Manitoba and Prince Edward Island. In June 1960 Quebec and New Brunswick, with Union Nationale and Conservative governments respectively, held elections. In New Brunswick, the Liberals, under Louis Robichaud, an Acadian, won a narrow victory. In Quebec, Jean Lesage's Liberals won by a nose. And Lesage's victory meant trouble for Diefenbaker.

Premier Maurice Duplessis had ruled his province with an iron hand since 1944. The Union Nationale machine regularly dispensed patronage out of its "caisse electorale" for its clients. Its general policy, which commended itself to wealthy and conservative individuals in English Montreal as well as to the average lower-middle-class, small-town voter who provided Duplessis with the backbone of his support, was socially conservative and ideologically reactionary. The government was run by "le chef," but not by le chef alone. When Duplessis died, in September 1959, he was succeeded by Paul Sauvé, his most prominent and independent-minded colleague. Sauvé died in his turn, however, on New Year's Day, 1960. The next premier, Antonio Barrette, was a product of the Union Nationale machine, and of very doubtful abilities. In the election of 1960, the Union Nationale slogan, "Les trois grands" (two of the three were already dead) was little match for the much more contemporary "Lesage s'engage" of the Liberals.

Lesage's success signalled much more than an ordinary electoral turnover. No longer could Diefenbaker count on a congenial government in Quebec City for political support. The electoral position of the Conservatives from Quebec at

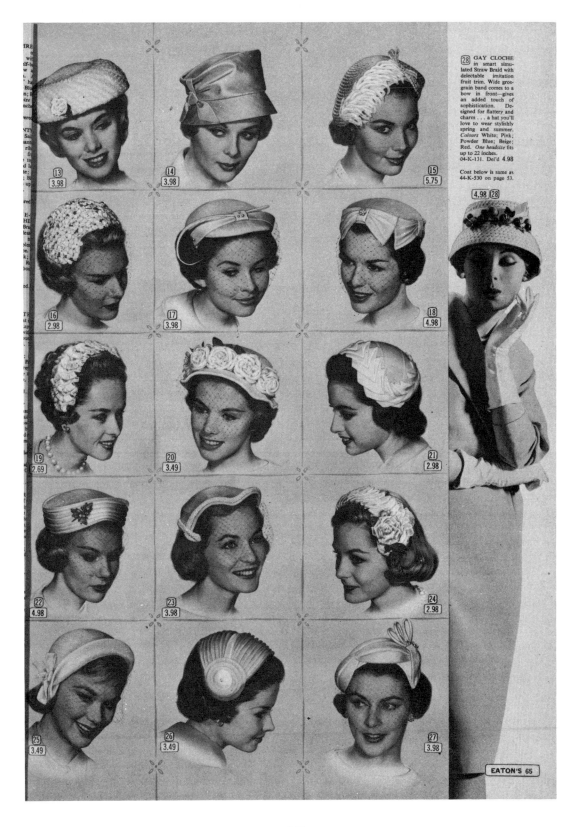

28 GAY CLOCHE in smart simulated Straw Braid with delectable imitation fruit trim. Wide gros-grain band comes to a bow in front—gives an added touch of sophistication. De-signed for flattery and charm . . . a hat you'll love to wear stylishly spring and summer. *Colours* White; Pink; Powder Blue; Beige; Red. *One headsize* fits up to 22 inches. 04-K-131. Del'd 4.98

Coat below is same as 44-K-530 on page 53.

4.98 28

13
3.98

14
3.98

15
5.75

16
2.98

17
3.98

18
4.98

19
2.69

20
3.49

21
2.98

22
4.98

23
3.98

24
2.98

25
3.49

26
3.49

27
3.98

EATON'S 65

Howard Green, Secretary of State for External Affairs, 1959-1963.
Public Archives Canada, PA-47150.

Ottawa was undermined. Weak in their original support, they could now do little to prevent their own political demise.

While the corners of the Conservative edifice were crumbling, there were as yet few telling attacks on Diefenbaker's conduct of the nation's business. An opening was provided by the Governor of the Bank of Canada, James Coyne. Coyne advocated a reduction in the inflow of foreign capital into Canada on the grounds that the country was living beyond its means. His views did not commend themselves either to bankers or to economists. Indeed, in December 1960 a group of seventeen economists petitioned finance minister

Donald Fleming to dismiss Coyne for incompetence. The government did not act immediately, but soon they found Coyne's public pronouncements so embarrassing that he was asked to refrain from further controversy. Finally, at the end of May 1961, Coyne was asked to resign.

The government was certainly within its rights in asking for Coyne's resignation, since even the most exalted of public servants is obliged to agree, in public at least, with the policies of his elected ministers. Usually such resignations are cloaked in principle, or justified for reasons of health. Coyne, however, was informed that the government was displeased with a recent increase in the Governor's pension, passed by the board of the Bank. Fleming claimed that he had known nothing of the increase. Coyne argued that he must have known, or at least had the opportunity to know. He repudiated any imputation that he might be feathering his own nest. Coyne now interpreted the demand for his resignation as an attack on his personal honour, and refused to resign. The government was forced to introduce a bill into the House of Commons declaring Coyne's office vacant. The bill duly passed the Commons on the wings of Diefenbaker's Parliamentary majority, and came to rest in the Senate.

The prototype of the ill-fated Canadian designed and built Arrow supersonic fighter plane on display in 1958. Cancellation of the Arrow program resulted in a major controversy. Five Arrows had been built and flown, but unfortunately none were preserved. Only fragments of the famous plane survive in museums. *Aviation and Space Division, National Museum of Science and Technology, Ottawa, Canada.*

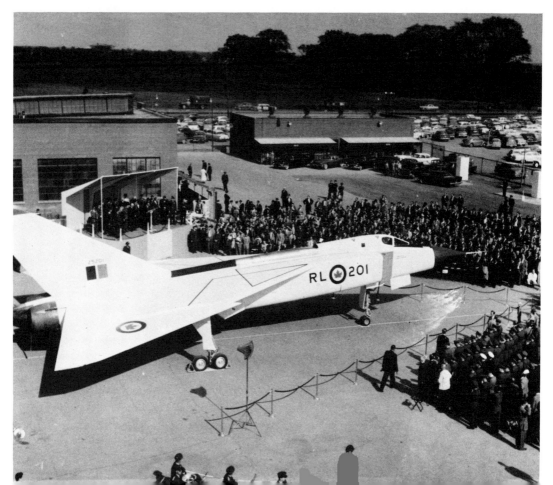

Walter Gordon, whose
eighteen months as
Minister of Finance
produced problems for
Pearson.
Public Archives Canada,
PA-110220. Capital Press.

The Senate usually defers to the elected chamber. From time to time, it exercises its undoubted prerogative to reject bills sent up from the House, and this possibility is increased if the Senate is dominated by the opposition. The Senate had been well stocked by Mackenzie King and St. Laurent, and still possessed, in 1961, an overwhelming Liberal majority. The Coyne case was being interpreted in the press as a case of individual injustice, and the Liberal senators decided that this was an issue on which they could defy the government. A Senate committee provided Coyne with a forum in which to defend his character and his views. The whole Senate then defeated the government's bill. Coyne, as he had promised to do, promptly resigned, his character and reputation vindicated. The government's character and reputation suffered accordingly.

The Coyne affair provided an ironic apostrophe to one of Diefenbaker's proudest achievements, the Canadian Bill

of Rights. Diefenbaker had championed the rights of individuals throughout his career and after the Second World War had condemned in Parliament the treatment meted out to Japanese Canadians during the conflict. In 1960 a Bill of Rights was passed setting out the general rights of Canadian citizens. Although, as was pointed out at the time, its application waited upon the courts, it seemed to be a notable advance in civil liberties. Now the Coyne affair, in which the government had been the victim of hapless circumstance, made Diefenbaker's majority seem as oppressive as the Liberals' had been in 1956. Just as the Liberals had lost the war of illusions in 1956, the Conservatives lost it in 1961.

The question arose: Would the Liberals be able to exploit the opportunity that was now offered? When a new Liberal MP, Judy LaMarsh, arrived in Ottawa in 1960, she found her fellow-Liberals "sunk in the deepest and most hopeless depression." They were still a party of losers, over-awed by the size of the majority that confronted them. In the same year, outside Parliament, the Liberals were beginning to pick themselves up. A Liberal Summer Conference was convened in Kingston, and there, for the first time, the Liberals displayed their new team to replace the vanished old guard of the 1950s. Tom Kent, a tall, scholarly Englishman, Walter Gordon, a Toronto accountant and one of Pearson's oldest friends, Mitchell Sharp, the former Deputy Minister of Trade and Commerce, all showed up. Gordon's economic nationalism and inclination towards social welfare combined with Kent's policy

Tom Kent, here photographed as Director of the Special Planning Secretariat, Privy Council Office.
Public Archives Canada, PA-110218. Capital Press.

proposals to give the impression that what was called "small-l liberalism" (as opposed to the business-oriented Howe-St. Laurent kind), was now dominant in the Liberal party.

The Kingston conference was important in itself, but it helped that it coincided with the refounding of the Social Credit Party (which had been wiped out in 1958) and preceded the transformation of the old CCF into the New Democratic Party, which was immediately baptized the "NDP." The NDP hoped to attract a broader range of voters than the old CCF had. It wanted the liberally-inclined middle class to switch from the "old parties" to its new social democratic platform. At the head of the NDP was placed the CCF's most successful and most attractive politician, Premier Tommy Douglas of Saskatchewan. Douglas' position was pre-empted by the signs of a leftward Liberal drift, which helped to keep potential voters in the fold. "Change," Pearson told the Kingston Conference, "is the essence of Liberalism."

By 1960 Pearson had mastered most of the skills required of the modern Canadian party leader: indefatigable oratory, a flexible disposition, and a cast-iron stomach. He knew, however, that he could not hope to match Diefenbaker as an orator, and he also knew that some considered his low-key personality to be a liability to the party. Although this was a deflating piece of information, he persevered in welding together a new version of the old Liberal party, travelling 60 000 miles in the pre-election year of 1961, shoring up party supporters across the country.

When Diefenbaker dissolved Parliament and called a general election for June 18, 1962, it was unthinkable that his political revolution could be reversed. There were encouraging signs for the Liberals. They were ahead in the public opinion polls, and had been for a year. The party was well-organized if not well-financed. The party had a platform, but the platform was not easily converted into an election issue with a strong impact on the electorate. In a year in which "modern," new American-style political gimmicks were the rage, the Liberals tried some, with very mixed results. Public opinion polls showed that the issue most worrying the electorate was unemployment, and on this issue the government's record was judged to be weakest. Liberal speakers therefore concentrated on the government's management of the economy. Stung, Diefenbaker and his ministers replied, and unemployment, a subject on which the public mind was already made up, became a major issue in the campaign.

Further apparent evidence of Conservative economic

mismanagement was provided by the devaluation of the Canadian dollar. The dollar had been at a premium in terms of U.S. dollars for some years, and Canadians took perverse pride that their dollar was worth more than the American variety. In fact, an overvalued Canadian dollar meant overpriced Canadian exports and harmed the Canadian economy. A devaluation was long overdue, and it was the government's policy to let the dollar drift downwards relative to the American dollar. The unresolved question was where the decline would stop, and statements by government ministers made it appear as if the government itself was divided on the question. By late May an exchange crisis was building up, and the Canadian dollar was under considerable pressure in world markets.

Irrationally, the electorate blamed the government for what was perceived as a decline in Canada's status abroad. "What's wrong with Canada?" Americans were reported as

Mitchell Sharp, who was Pearson's Minister of Finance after the resignation of Walter Gordon.
Public Archives Canada, PA-110221.

On September 1, 1937, a
few weeks after Pearson
had been deeply involved
in the complicated
arrangements for Canada's
participation in the

Coronation and in the
Imperial Conference in
London, Trans-Canada
Airlines carried their first
paying passengers. They
travelled in a 10-passenger

Lockheed plane similar
to the one pictured above.
By the time Pearson
retired, Air Canada was
flying a fleet of jetliners,
such as the Lockheed

below. The change
in name had become
effective on January 1,
1965.
Air Canada Photo.

An early portrait of M. J. Coldwell, leader of the CCF, 1940-1958. Pearson had him appointed to the Privy Council in 1964.
Archives of Saskatchewan.

asking. For urban voters, Diefenbaker was not the man to give the answer. But in rural areas and in the west, the Conservatives put up a hard fight. Pearson and the Liberals were "a cesspool of civil servants with red friends," one western Tory charged. In the flurry of Diefenbaker-versus-Pearson politics, commentators ignored one totally new and unexpected development.

A car salesman from Rouyn, Quebec, Réal Caouette, was stumping rural Quebec with the message, "You've got nothing to lose" — why not vote Social Credit? His rural audiences agreed. Too late, the Liberals discovered that Quebec would not simply switch back from Diefenbaker. The Liberals' popular provincial cabinet minister, René Lévesque, was thrown into the fray, but nothing could now save the situation.

When the election news came in, the Liberals did well

in cities across the country, except in the prairies. In Quebec, they advanced from 25 to 35 seats, but both Liberals and Conservatives lost rural seats to the Social Crediters. Even some suburban and urban ridings fell to the Creditistes, and among the fallen was Pearson's friend and economic adviser, Maurice Lamontagne.

The result was a Parliament of minorities. Diefenbaker lost his majority, falling from 208 supporters to 116. The Social Crediters had 30, 26 from Quebec, and the NDP had 19. The Liberals emerged with 99 seats — not the hoped-for victory, but not a defeat either. Despite the fact that they had won

Tommy Douglas speaking in 1961 at the founding convention of the New Democratic Party (the NDP), which elected him its first leader.
Public Archives Canada, C-36219.

Enjoying baseball—a
lifelong enthusiasm which
he shared with his father—
at Kingston in 1962.
Public Archives Canada,
C-90354.

17 fewer seats than the Conservatives, the Liberals marginally outpolled them in popular vote.

For Diefenbaker the election was a catastrophe. He had, it was true, salvaged the party from the certain defeat indicated by the polls to a plurality of seats in Parliament. Nevertheless, his government had been severely battered by the electorate, several ministers had been defeated, and he had lost control of the House of Commons. The impending financial crisis, with an international run on the Canadian dollar, broke within days of the election. Immediate austerity measures were taken, and these too did not reflect well on the government. A close friend was killed in an automobile accident, and Diefenbaker broke his ankle. The summer was spent in an atmosphere of profound gloom and inactivity.

Parliament reassembled on September 27. The Liberal strategy was to delay, obstruct and to seek to find an issue on which the three opposition parties could unite to defeat the government. The Conservatives, obviously, wanted to find a way to postpone this eventuality, or to avoid it altogether. October passed in Parliamentary skirmishing, but the government remained in office. With a Christmas recess impending, it seemed as if Diefenbaker had weathered the worst of the storm.

Two developments in the fall of 1962 helped to bring matters to a head. In Quebec, Lesage dissolved the legislature and went to his electorate on the issue of nationalizing Quebec's private electric power companies. His chosen slogan was "maîtres chez nous," a phrase which certainly applied to the main issue, but which in fact went much farther. "Maîtres chez nous" was a call for the awakening of Quebec, a summons for its liberation from domination by "les autres" — by private business, or, just conceivably, by English Canada. Lesage won his election, but it was becoming clear to English Canadians that all was not well in Quebec. Maurice Lamontagne pressed Pearson to take action, to say something that would show that Quebec would get a sympathetic hearing from the Liberals. In response, Pearson decided to adopt a suggestion made by the editor of the Montreal newspaper, *Le Devoir*, André Laurendeau: a royal commission to investigate cultural and linguistic disparities between the English and French language groups in Canada. Pearson proposed such a commission in a speech in Parliament on December 17, and scored an immediate success in French Canada. Even Pierre Sévigny, a Conservative minister, approved. Diefenbaker, however, said nothing.

When Pearson delivered himself of his bilingual pronouncement, there was no evidence that he would be called on in the immediate future to make good his promise. Diefenbaker had survived the storms of autumn and had beaten back the worst that the opposition parties could throw at him. What Pearson and Diefenbaker could not know was that the next threat to the Diefenbaker government would come from within the Prime Minister's own party. Within a month, the Diefenbaker government would be approaching dissolution because of a long-postponed issue in defence policy.

OPPOSITE
The BOMARC missile. This American missile was selected by Diefenbaker for defence against Russian invasion of Canadian home territory. It became central to the controversial issues of nuclear weapons for Canada and Canada's defence role in relations between the Soviet Union and the United States. *Canadian Forces Photo.*

116

In 1959, when Diefenbaker had cancelled the Arrow, he had opted instead for the American CF-104 fighter to equip the Canadian air division in Europe. For home defence against Russian bombers, he selected the American-made BOMARC missile. The BOMARC and the CF-104 were intended to be equipped with nuclear weapons which, under the arrangements then prevailing, would be stored under joint Canadian-American control until needed. But the acquisition of nuclear weapons, even in this diluted form, was a lively political issue in Canada. The mass media had repeatedly stressed the horrors of a nuclear war, and the path of prudence and virtue seemed to be to keep nuclear weapons at arm's length. Some publicists went further and demanded that Canada become neutral in the global struggle between the United States and the USSR. Much was made of the leadership role which Canada could assume vis-à-vis the underdeveloped nations (the later third world) which were just then achieving independence. Within the cabinet, the cause of disarmament and distance from the United States was pleaded by the external affairs minister, Howard Green; the Minister of National Defence, Douglas Harkness, argued the other side.

Matters were brought to a head by the second major political event of the fall of 1962, the Cuban missile crisis. Diefenbaker was informed, but not consulted, about the American decision to blockade Cuba to force the removal of Russian missiles being installed there. Diefenbaker refused to announce an automatic alert for Canada's armed forces and in his public statements did not enthusiastically support the American action. Defence minister Harkness, however, seems to have put Canadian forces on an alert. Diefenbaker's unwillingness to back the United States attracted widespread criticism in Canada and outside, and it seemed to bring into focus the incoherent defence policy that the Conservative government had hitherto followed.

Until the fall of 1962 the Liberals had taken the fashionable position of opposing the acquisition of nuclear weapons. Pearson was widely criticized for telling a television audience, in response to one of the stock questions of the day, that he would rather be "red than dead," although he emphasized that he would go on fighting communism. Mrs. Pearson joined the Voice of Women, an organization opposing the spread of nuclear weapons. Late in 1962, however, Pearson was approached by Paul Hellyer, the Liberals' defence critic in the House of Commons. Hellyer told Pearson that it was his understanding that the Diefenbaker government was not honouring Canada's defence commitments in its persistent refusal to acquire nuclear warheads for weapons already in the Canadian arsenal. In December, Hellyer and Charles Drury, the former Deputy Minister of National Defence and now a Liberal MP, made speeches advocating a change of policy for the party and the country: Canada must acquire nuclear weapons to be an effective ally.

The next Liberal to reverse himself was Pearson. In a speech in the Toronto suburb of Scarborough, on January 12, 1963, Pearson told his Liberal audience that he was ashamed, "as a Canadian . . . if we accept nuclear commitments and then refuse to discharge them." Canada, he added, could only discharge its commitments "by accepting nuclear warheads."

Pearson's change of front took many Liberals by surprise. It proved to be intensely unpopular in intellectual circles. The editor of a "small l liberal" Montreal magazine, Pierre-Elliott Trudeau, spoke for many when he denounced Pearson as "the unfrocked pope of peace." While a few Liberals on the party's left wing deserted Pearson on the issue, a large section of the electorate was reassured by Pearson's promise that a Liberal government would honour Canada's international commitments, and restore Canada's position with its allies. The inevitable Gallup poll revealed that most Canadians agreed with Pearson.

When Parliament reassembled later that month, it was evident that the disagreements within the cabinet could not be papered over much longer. Diefenbaker, Green and Harkness continued at loggerheads inside the cabinet and then, for the first time, in public. They issued conflicting statements. One by Diefenbaker provoked an acerbic American response, in the form of a State Department press release, which confirmed that in the Americans' opinion Canada was indeed not fulfilling its international obligations.

The final act began with Harkness' resignation on February 4. That same day, Pearson moved in the House of Commons "that this government, because of lack of leadership, the breakdown of unity in the cabinet, and confusion and indecision in dealing with national and international problems, does not have the confidence of the Canadian people." Dramatic as were the events on the floor of the House, where at last the fall of the government seemed an imminent probability, they were overshadowed by the comings and goings of cliques and cabals within the Conservative cabinet and caucus. Last-ditch negotiations were begun with the Social Credit Party, which held the margin of victory or defeat in

OPPOSITE
Quebec Liberal
Convention, Montreal,
February 23, 1963.
Public Archives Canada,
C-31797.

the House of Commons for the government. Diefenbaker refused to compromise with the Social Crediters. That group proposed an amendment to Pearson's motion which for once omitted all mention of the party's monetary nostrums, thereby making it possible for other parties to vote for it. And so it was on a Social Credit motion that the Diefenbaker government fell, 142 to 111. The vote on the Liberal motion followed, with the same result, on February 5, 1963. Diefenbaker dissolved Parliament, and an election was called for April 8.

The imminence of an election added a desperate element to the ongoing conspiracies within the Conservative Party. On February 9 Walter Gordon announced to a cheering Liberal convention that George Hees and Pierre Sévigny had just resigned from the cabinet, alleging that Diefenbaker intended to run an anti-American campaign in the coming election. With the Conservatives disintegrating and the Liberals far out in front in the public opinion polls, it seemed as if Pearson and his party would soon return in glory to the seats they had vacated in 1957.

The Liberals had also been ahead in the polls in 1962. In the aftermath of the failure to exploit their initial margin in that election, some commentators expressed grave doubts as to Pearson's ability to keep his supporters firmly behind him. Diefenbaker, by contrast, campaigned consistently ahead of his party. In 1963 he concentrated on his bastions of proven strength: the prairies, the countryside, and the small cities. Toronto, which was abandoning its old "tory blue" for Liberal red, was left strictly alone.

Pearson once more went through his paces as a party leader in quest of the voter. He cheerfully submitted to the campaign rituals, which this time, as in 1958, included all the inconveniences of the Canadian winter. While he could be a graceful and charming speaker on relaxed occasions, large public meetings were not his forte. What was intended as forceful oratory came across, more often than not, as a modified, high-pitched splutter. Nevertheless, Pearson's speaking tour was a success, and never more than when he succeeded in facing down a howling mob in Vancouver. The chosen weapon of the Vancouver rowdies was pea-shooters, and while Pearson ploughed manfully through his text for forty-five minutes, peas were bouncing off his head. Afterwards Pearson's organizers congratulated the leader on a splendid performance. Fortitude in ordeals obviously won votes. The extension of this political rule was difficult to contemplate. The Liberal campaign culminated in a serio-comic rally in Maple Leaf Gardens in Toronto where the Liberal hero marched in behind drum majorettes to the strains of the march from the movie *Ben Hur*.

On April 8 the Liberals won 129 seats, four short of a majority, the Conservatives 95, the Socreds 24, and the NDP 19. The cities voted massively for Pearson and the Liberals. In metropolitan Toronto, Montreal and Vancouver the Conservatives kept only one seat. In other cities they did almost as badly. But the prairies held firm for Diefenbaker. Pearson's victory was not only not complete, but was regional in nature. The Liberals emerged as the party of the urban east, centre and far west. It was an ominous sign.

5
Lights and Shadows

ON APRIL 22, 1963, Pearson and twenty-five Liberal colleagues arrived at Rideau Hall to take the oath of office from Governor General George Vanier. It was the largest cabinet in Canadian history, and the collective qualifications of its members were impressive, although, it perhaps did not deserve the lavish description of "the most impressive array of brains ever assembled in a Canadian cabinet," bestowed by an over-enthusiastic political scientist. Nonetheless, the brains would soon have to be put to strenuous work in mastering the problems of a complex and steadily proliferating governmental organization. And, of course, Pearson had promised to set Canada back on the right track.

The country that the Liberals confronted had changed since the fifties. Canada had more people, over 18 000 000 in 1961 compared to the 14 000 000 of 1951. The Gross National Product, the favoured index of economic growth, had increased considerably, despite the various recessions, to over $42 billion in 1962 from about $35 billion in 1957 (measured in constant dollars). This quantitative growth was gratifying to those given to admiring large statistics. It also helped to stimulate demands that this large increase in national wealth, that had made Canadians per capita the second-richest nation on earth, should be used to alleviate domestic misery, and to give Canadians more security against misfortune.

The economic hardship of the years since 1957 had accentuated these demands. Luckily for Pearson, his administration coincided with a return of prosperity and a drop in the unemployment statistics. The change in the economic climate had come too late to be perceived by the electorate, although the Conservatives had vainly tried to draw attention to it. Unemployment was down, and continued to drop: 5.5% in 1963, 4.7% in 1964, 3.9% in 1965, down to a low of 3.6%

OPPOSITE
Parliament Hill on July 1, 1967, when Her Majesty the Queen participated in the centennial celebrations. *Malak Photographs Limited.*

125

in 1966, while the labour force, reflecting the baby boom of the post-war years, grew by almost a million. Relative economic prosperity and tenure of office are always happy coincidences, and Canada in the sixties and the Pearson government were both fortunate in that regard.

The Canadian economy was expanding as unemployment went down. Investment funds were required, and the government, with more qualms than its predecessors in the fifties, regarded continuing American investment as an ingredient in that expansion. It was in any case debatable whether this meant that there was an increasing reliance on foreign investment. Thus, when the American government for its own purposes contemplated restrictions that threatened to cut off the golden flow, Canada protested and secured a special exemption.

Not all investment went into capital goods for industry. A considerable amount of public funds was devoted to the ordinary needs and tasks of a growing country, and the result, by the early 1960s, was a rapidly changing landscape as cities grew and suburbs swallowed up farmland. In some parts of Ontario, for example, it was estimated that 148 acres of improved farmland were lost for every thousand increase in urban population. Unhappily, expanding cities were often situated in the middle of prime agricultural land (the Niagara fruit belt and the lower Fraser valley are examples), and the indiscriminate expansion of cities therefore appeared to threaten the cities' local food supply as well as a large proportion of Canada's fruit crop.

The suburbs grew steadily. Urban planners had a field day as the planned self-contained community made its appearance: Don Mills, a Toronto suburb; Elliot Lake, a northern Ontario mining town; Kitimat, a British Columbia city centred on an aluminum smelter. For shopping, the "shopping centre" was devised, or rather imported from the United States, to concentrate a wide variety of shopping facilities, from groceries to shoes, in the suburban neighbourhood. This development in its turn prompted fears that another American phenomenon, the decay of the central core of cities, might spread to Canada. Although Canada did not escape entirely, the fate of the Canadian cities was happier than that of some in the United States.

Downtown, office towers and shopping complexes spread out of their pre-war quarters. A British traveller, viewing Toronto in 1960, wandered "up and down University Avenue, looking in vain for a familiar landmark of war-time days. I

OPPOSITE
A glimpse of the emotion-filled ceremony on Parliament Hill on February 15, 1965, when the old ensign was lowered and the new Canadian flag was hoisted for the first time.
Public Archives Canada, C-1204.

Pearson "signing in" as
Prime Minister in 1963.
*Public Archives Canada,
PA-110782. Capital Press.*

found none; gone were the low, higgledy-piggledy, private dwellings – in their place serried ranks of imposing glass and concrete buildings." This was admittedly rather dull, but in Toronto that was mitigated by the fact that it "has never been famed for its architectural delights." In Montreal the downtown was encroached upon by even larger "glass and concrete buildings," including underground shopping malls – a practical answer to the city's abominable winter climate.

To serve the new downtown business cities, arterial roads

were cut through old urban areas and four-, six-, and finally twelve-lane highways encircled Canada's larger cities. Premier Lesage pragmatically dubbed Montreal's Metropolitan Boulevard part of the Trans-Canada Highway and collected federal grants for it, thereby combining provincial necessities with federal priorities in an eminently practical and lucrative way. Toronto opened its subway in 1954 — Canada's first — and Montreal followed in 1967. For public transit, it was the age of the bus and the subway. Streetcars were a casualty of the

Interruption during the 1963 annual baseball game on Parliament Hill.
Public Archives Canada, C-90460.

Simon Fraser University, near Vancouver, enrolled its first students in the fall of 1965. Its impressive buildings symbolized both the advances made in Canadian architecture and the great expansion of facilities for higher education that took place during the Pearson era. *Simon Fraser University*.

period as cities scrambled to rid themselves of forms of transit regarded as obsolete. Only later was it recognized that street-cars, with their rights of way, could have helped to solve later problems of mass transportation. Long years later, Canadian visitors to Brazil were surprised to find the unmistakable traces of the platform for the indoor stove on Brazilian streetcars — an indirect result of the scrapping of most of Canada's electric railways.

Where the streetcar had gone, another Canadian, or at least English-Canadian, tradition followed: the liquor laws. Since the 1920s, Canadians had suffered various forms of in-convenience to get a drink. If a citizen took a drink on his porch, for example, he was subject to prosecution. In Prince Edward Island he could not get a drink at all — legally. It was suggested that the Islanders paid less than passing attention to this law, especially around elections, and it therefore primarily

inconvenienced tourists. Finally, in a 1959 speech, one visitor to Canada, the Duke of Edinburgh, complained loudly and, no doubt, from bitter experience. It was a sign of the times. Within the next decade even Prince Edward Island had succumbed to fashion and abolished prohibition.

Fashion was insidiously creeping into most Canadian households. Rural electrification, unknown in some areas of the country in 1945, was virtually complete by the 1960s. Sewage projects, halted by bankrupt municipalities during the depression, were resumed, and the backyard privy went into an irreversible decline. Electricity brought television, at first over the border from American stations, and then from stations within Canada itself. As a result, thousands of Canadians watched enthralled as Queen Elizabeth II was crowned on June 2, 1953. Soon live drama (a short-lived phenomenon), the news with Larry Henderson, the CBC's first television

Place Ville Marie, Montreal. One of the first large-scale developments of its kind in Canada, it demonstrated in a spectacular way the impact that the new international style was having on architecture in Canada. The downtown areas of Montreal, Toronto, Ottawa, Vancouver, and other Canadian cities, were in great measure rebuilt in the fifties and sixties, and high-rises, both business and residential, transformed their skylines. *Ministère du Tourisme, de la Chasse et de la Pêche, Québec.*

news personality, and Hockey Night in Canada were national institutions. Worried nationalists and believers in "high culture" noted with concern and then alarm that Canadians had an apparently insatiable appetite for American television serials. Naturally, most concern was directed at the possible effect of television on children, and soon scholarly studies were rolling off the presses on the impact of television on reading habits and general literacy.

Other gadgets besides television invaded the home. Refrigerators, although common enough before the war in the homes of the middle class, became commonplace in the decade following 1945. One study at the end of the 1950s argued that a Canadian housewife need only spend one hour and thirty-six minutes a day preparing the family meals, compared to five and a half hours in the 1920s. To this were added the convenience of supermarket shopping and often the availability of a car for transport.

Rural life was inevitably less convenient, although much easier than in earlier generations. Young men and women continued to drift away from farms, attracted by the higher wages and better conditions offered in the cities. In 1956, the average net farm income was only $1090, compared with $1350 for all other industries. In 1957, the year in which the farm voter turned away from C. D. Howe and the Liberals, the president of the Canadian Federation of Agriculture pointedly remarked that "the farmer sees an era of unprecedented prosperity by-passing the farm."

This was partly true, but only in relative terms. Some farmers were simply cultivating marginal or sub-marginal land, and under Diefenbaker, policies were devised to move farmers off uneconomic farms. On viable farms, the wheat sales of the early 1960s improved matters considerably, and even before the wheat sales, increased mechanization had made the process of sowing and harvesting considerably less laborious. Nor were all farmers deprived — even in the fifties, the habit of boarding up the farm and heading south for a winter vacation was spreading.

Sometimes fortuitous events had an effect. A national rail strike in 1950 forced shippers to think of alternatives to their traditional reliance on railways. Much of the business that was lost that year to trucks never came back, and trucking began to threaten not simply the monopoly of railways on freight haulage, but their profitability, and then their very existence. Passenger travel on the railways declined as well, as long-haul passengers began to desert to airlines, and the short-haul ones to buses. The railways attempted to fight back with first-class transcontinental trains, like the CPR's "Canadian," but theirs was a losing battle.

It was in the railways in the late 1950s that traditional

The opening of the Macdonald-Cartier interprovincial bridge across the Ottawa River in 1965—one of numerous important highway improvements completed in the sixties. Pearson officiated along with Jean Lesage (left), Premier of Quebec, and John Robarts, Premier of Ontario. *Public Archives Canada, C-90479.*

Scarborough, Toronto's neighbour to the east, photographed from Victoria Park in 1949 and in 1969. The later view illustrates the spectacular suburban growth that took place in areas adjacent to Canada's large cities in the two decades.
G. H. Jarrett. Northway Survey Corporation Limited.

forms of employment came face to face with the developments of technology. The railways, by the late 1950s, had switched from steam to diesel engines. This jeopardized the jobs of firemen on yard engines, since the railways were unwilling to employ a superfluous work force indefinitely. A strike, and then a compromise, gradually phasing out the firemen, followed. But "technological unemployment" remained a source of acute anxiety for men and women who, through no fault of their own, were left behind in the race for improving technology.

An age of greater leisure also took its toll of traditional

Urban expansion above and below ground was characteristic of Canada during the 1960s. Here, Lester Pearson, sharing a seat with his brother Vaughan, is joined by Metro Chairman William R. Allen for a ride on the

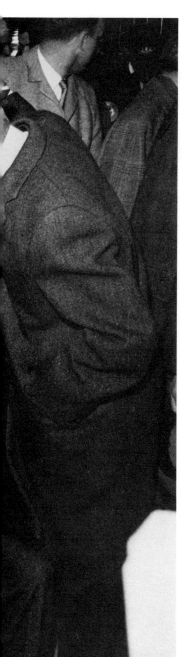

forms of recreation. The "pop star" was already an established fact in the 1940s, but what was new was a moneyed, leisured, and more and more plentiful class of teenagers, the "youth market," to which the entertainment industry could appeal. The astonishing career of Elvis Presley in the mid-1950s established rock and roll as the dominant musical form. Along with Elvis' records came his blue-suede shoes, his clothing and even his duck-tailed haircut. After Presley, the Beatles came in the mid-1960s, another international musical phenomenon, bringing their styles and paraphernalia.

Canada had its own musical heroes — Paul Anka and Bobby Curtola — but their songs and styles were hardly particularly Canadian. Had they directed their appeal to Canadian audiences on Canadian themes their careers would likely have been short ones, even in their native land. For youthful styles were becoming well-nigh universal, from San Diego to Bucharest, passing through Flin Flon and Chicoutimi on the way.

A revolution in taste accompanied the youth cult, as older generations strove to understand the younger, and tried to regain their own youth in the process. "Youthful" styles spread upward. Long hair and beards reappeared, beginning in the mid-sixties. Short skirts were exhumed from the twenties, and then grew shorter than they had ever been in the twenties. Religion, which had seemed to be immovably entrenched in the 1950s, went out of fashion in the 1960s. The Catholic Church, the bastion of conservative religion and strict moral teaching, liberalized itself in the Second Vatican Council of 1962, with Canada's Cardinal Léger playing a prominent part. The strain proved too much for many Catholics. Instead of gratifying the faithful, the change perturbed them. For others, it was not enough. Catholic church attendance, even in Quebec, declined, while resignations from religious orders, previously comparatively rare and unnoticed, soon threatened many of the Church's institutions. Protestant sects also suffered a decline during the 1960s, except among the pentecostal sects where membership grew.

Among Roman Catholics, one ostensible reason for discontent was the Church's continuing refusal to countenance any form of artificial birth control. But just as the Church was preparing for the Vatican Council, the easiest form of contraceptive yet was put on the market: the Pill. The consequences for the Church were apparently serious. The consequences for the Canadian birth rate were catastrophic. In Quebec, the most Catholic province of all, the birth rate per

137

Television broadcasting in Canada began in September 1952, in Montreal and Toronto. The CBC nationwide network was completed in 1958. In those early days few foresaw the profound effect TV would have on politics, and on Canadian life generally. These cumbersome early TV receivers were displayed at the Canadian National Exhibition, in Toronto.
Public Archives Canada, PA-52964.

thousand sank from an average of 22 in the early 1950s to an astounding 9.6 in 1968 – lower than Ontario's. Henceforth Canada's population began, on the average, to age, except insofar as immigration restored the balance. Most immigrants chose to speak English as it was the most practical language from their point of view. With the Quebec birth rate no longer compensating for immigration, the traditional demographic balance in Canada was altered to the evident disadvantage of French-speaking Canadians.

Inevitably, politics lags behind cultural and social developments, and Canada's political life during the 1960s did not immediately reflect the social, intellectual, or even moral developments of the decade. With Pearson's arrival in office, however, one age-old Canadian custom did come to an end: the death penalty. The death penalty was prescribed by law for murder and treason and under Mackenzie King, St. Laurent and Diefenbaker, the federal cabinet had had to sit as a tribunal of last resort to determine whether the royal prerogative of mercy ought to be exercised on a condemned man, and the sentence of death commuted to that of life imprisonment. In December 1962 two murderers were hanged in Toronto's Don Jail while a crowd of opponents of capital punishment demonstrated outside the prison. Under Pearson, the royal prerogative was invariably exercised and the hangings of 1962 were the last.

Pearson's decision not to send anyone else to the gallows was arguably a genuinely "liberal" act, as liberalism was understood in the 1960s. It sustained humanitarian values and sought to abolish cruel or useless hangovers from the past. Pearson intended to apply these values in other areas as well.

The foundation of the exercise of power was the Liberals' near-majority in the House of Commons. The 129 Liberal members were a fairly talented group, with plenty of cabinet material among them. Inevitably, some members of the cabinet were foreordained. The survivors of the St. Laurent cabinet, Martin, Chevrier, Pickersgill and Hellyer marched back into office. Harry Hays, the new Liberal member for Calgary South and the only Liberal elected in Alberta or Saskatchewan, became Minister of Agriculture. Walter Gordon, Pearson's old friend and steady supporter in opposition, became Minister of Finance, although not without some apparent misgivings on Pearson's part.

1952 Motorola television set.
Public Archives Canada, PA-77934. The Gazette, *Montreal.*

Wayne and Shuster, later famous for their TV specials, made their television debut in French-English comedy in October 1953.
Public Archives Canada, PA-77927. The Gazette, Montreal.

Pearson's own office was run by his secretary of many years, Mary Macdonald, while Tom Kent moved into the East Block as Pearson's chief policy adviser. Pearson also drew on the advice and support of an astonishing number of friends across the country, and was daily bombarded with "Dear Mike" letters proffering advice, both good and bad, on the future of the country.

During the campaign Pearson had promised "Sixty Days of Decision" to replace the "fumble-bumble" of the last days

of Diefenbaker. Now he had to produce. Parliament was summoned as soon as possible to witness and ratify the return to confident and efficient Liberal administration.

The first major piece of legislation to come before Parliament was the budget, presented by Walter Gordon. Gordon was himself a symbol of the Liberal revival, and it was expected, not least by Gordon himself, that the budget would mark a turning point between the hesitant and contradictory policies of his predecessors and the new, progressive policies of the Liberals. In preparing his budget, Gordon had rejected a draft by his officials and had relied on advice from three outside consultants from Toronto, who were temporarily seconded from their firms for the purpose. Officials in the finance department were not pleased by this development, and Parliament was still more offended.

Gordon was an ardent nationalist and his budget, when

"The National," the CBC nationwide evening news broadcast, became an institution in the 1950s, when Larry Henderson, its announcer, became for a time the best known television personality in the country.
CBC.

Elvis Presley performing
at Maple Leaf Gardens,
Toronto.
Public Archives Canada,
C-35680.

presented to Parliament on June 13, contained several controversial proposals designed to implement his ideas about returning direct ownership of the Canadian economy to Canadians. These proposals had provoked some criticism from the Governor of the Bank of Canada even before the budget was presented, but it was nothing compared to the storm of abuse that descended afterwards. Canadian businessmen were scandalized and protested volubly, both to Gordon and to Pearson himself. According to the president of the Montreal Stock Exchange, Eric Kierans, "The financial capitals of the world have just about had enough from Canada." However hyperbolic Kierans' statement might have been, it was abundantly clear that the Canadian business community had already had more than enough from Walter Gordon.

As though business criticism were not enough, Gordon was attacked on another front. The outside consultants had come to the attention of his Parliamentary opposition. Here was an issue more easily grasped than takeover taxes: the possibility that outside interests had benefited in some unspecified way from the employment of outside consultants in the preparation of the most secret of all state papers, the national budget. Gordon sat unhappily in Parliament while his opponents read him solemn homilies on the necessity of treading the path of unquestionable propriety. It was too much for the already beleaguered minister. On June 19 Gordon withdrew his takeover tax for further study. The budget had been seriously damaged, and so had Liberal morale. The Liberals' bright Parliamentary star had turned out to be only a comet, and

Eager fans of the Beatles who are soon to appear at Toronto's Maple Leaf Gardens talk with radio DJ's Jungle Jay Nelson and Al Boliska.
Public Archives Canada, C-35670.

The grim old Don Jail in Toronto, where the last executions in Canada were carried out in 1962. Thereafter, until hanging was abolished by law, the Cabinet invariably commuted death sentences. *City of Toronto Archives, Salmon Collection #616.*

Gordon emerged a diminished politician. The opposition had tasted blood, and where one had gone others might follow.

The next problem for Pearson did not come so much from Parliament as from the provinces. Pearson had promised "co-operative federalism" in federal-provincial relations, but his happy phrase concealed a distressing reality. As the acute emergencies of the war and the cold war faded into the past, the provinces' responsibility for education and social services assumed more importance in the mind of the electorate. Pearson's Liberals had promised, and intended to deliver, more social security for the Canadian people. That would require the co-operation of the provinces, including nationalist Quebec and rich Ontario.

The first act of what later seemed an interminable federal-provincial soap opera, "The Perils of Pearson," centred on what became the Canada Pension Plan. The pension plan was designed to provide more adequate pensions for Canada's aged. Pearson's (or rather, the Department of Health and Welfare's) original scheme envisaged a contributory, largely compulsory, pension plan, whose benefits would be tied to the rise in the cost of living. The federal proposals were unveiled at a federal-provincial conference in July. Ontario, which had been toying with pensions for the past year, was uneasy. Quebec, however, was definitely hostile. Premier Lesage informed the startled federal delegation that his province intended to go it alone. Another "decisive" Liberal program faced obliteration. A further meeting in November produced no agreement, and in March, when Pearson and the premiers met in Quebec City with a mob of separatists demonstrating outside, it seemed as if Canada's mechanism of automatic compromise in politics had broken down entirely.

From behind Ottawa's intransigent position, a small feeler crept out to the Quebec side. Advised by Tom Kent, Pearson was reaching out for some possible compromise and with some good will from Quebec officials and Lesage, and

The mini. Inspired by the "London Look" which centered on the famous Carnaby Street, the miniskirt swept the fashion world. These examples appeared in *Chatelaine*, February 1969. *Metropolitan Toronto Library Board*.

agreement was finally reached. There would be two pension plans, Canada's and Quebec's, but they would have identical provisions. The two sides compromised on details, but the final package turned over the fruits of the Pension Plan contributions — a very large sum — to the provinces.

Pearson's political style showed to its best and worst advantage in the Pension Plan episode. The federal government had presented the provinces with a pension scheme which proved to be unacceptable to one vital province. It own pension scheme was, by general consent, inferior to Quebec's. A retreat was necessary, but not before political histrionics had created a crisis of national unity. Yet Pearson had navigated smoothly and the ship of state reached the harbour of safety. Few observed at the time that the accompanying tempest was largely self-generated.

Pensions, however important for the general welfare, are a difficult subject for press and public to sink their teeth into. No sooner was the pension plan assured than Pearson presented Canadians with a plainer issue: a national flag. On May 17, 1964, he told the national convention of the Canadian Legion that he was going to propose a resolution in Parliament pro-

The "Fathers of the Repatriated Constitution" in 1964. More than ten years later, this issue was still a lively one among the Prime Minister, the people, and the press. Back row, left to right: Shaw, Stanfield, Laing, Bennett, Smallwood, Robichaud, Gordon. Front row, left to right: Roblin, Robarts, Favreau, Pearson, Manning, Lesage.
Public Archives Canada, C-94169.

DAL TUO VOTO...

DIPENDERA' IL TUO FUTURO!
QUELLO DEL CANADA'!
E QUELLO DEI TUOI FIGLI!

vota solo **LIBERALE!**

Immigration reflected in politics: a poster in Italian used by the Liberals in the 1965 election campaign.
Metropolitan Toronto Library Board.

viding for a distinctive national flag. On June 5, he did just that. Pearson favoured a red-blue-white Canadian flag with red maple leaves in the centre on a white background, and blue bars symbolizing the seas on each side.

When the flag was presented to Parliament, it was obvious that the debate of the year was on. After exhaustive discussion, the flag was referred to a Parliamentary committee in September. When it emerged, by a vote of 11 to 4, it had lost its blue bars and two of its red maple leaves. Nonetheless, debate went on. Diefenbaker had decided to oppose the new flag to the last ditch of debate and no compromise was possible. If the govern-

Guy Rouleau, whose indiscretions reflected unfortunately on Guy Favreau, the Minister of Justice.
Public Archives Canada, PA-47602.

La direction
Libérale

Campaign '65.
*Metropolitan Toronto
Library Board.*

Pearson dons a hard hat
at Elliot Lake during the
1965 campaign.
*Public Archives Canada,
PA-110816.*

Pearson with Hellyer,
LaMarsh, Martin,
MacEachern and
Macdonald in a formal

group portrait of 1966.
Public Archives Canada,
C-90443.

ment introduced closure the magic precedent of the pipeline debate could be invoked, and once again the Liberals would be seen to be trampling on the rights of Parliament. But closure had originally been designed to put an end to interminable and pointless debate, and by early December the public was ready to accept such a measure. So were some of Diefenbaker's own followers. On December 9 Léon Balcer, the Conservative MP for Trois-Rivières, suggested that the government introduce closure, and on December 11 it did. At 2:13 a.m. on December

Her Majesty the Queen cutting the enormous 100th birthday cake on Parliament Hill.
Public Archives Canada, C-24559.

OPPOSITE
Perhaps the most talked-about building at Expo 67 — the United States pavilion. It was designed by Buckminster Fuller, a highly original and innovative architect and engineer, who devised the geodesic dome — a spherical structure made up of very light but immensely strong triangular members.
Gouvernement du Québec. Ministère du Tourisme, de la Chasse et de la Pêche.

Bobby Gimby, who composed the popular centennial song, leading a children's parade. *Public Archives Canada, C-26756.*

13, the House of Commons adopted the maple leaf flag by a vote of 163 to 78, disregarding appeals from Pearson not to have a recorded vote on the new national symbol.

On the appointed day, the fifteenth of February, 1965, the old Red Ensign was lowered for the last time over Parliament Hill and the new maple leaf flag rose into the bright sunshine, and Diefenbaker brushed away a tear. As the Pearsons walked back into the Centre Block, the crowd inside broke into spontaneous applause.

For Pearson it was a good day in a bad year. The bumbling, interminable flag debate had been a counterpoint to a series of minor scandals that damaged the Liberal government's reputation still further and led to what Pearson later called a situation of "politics in disrepute." Late in 1964, he felt obliged to dismiss his Parliamentary Secretary, Guy Rouleau, for involvement in interference with the prosecution of a gangster, Lucien Rivard, in Montreal. The ramifications went further, however, and touched the office of the Minister of Justice,

Guy Favreau, one of the most prominent and best-liked members of the cabinet. A judicial enquiry was held under Mr. Justice Frédéric Dorion. Dorion's report, which was issued in June 1965, criticized not Favreau's personal integrity, which was beyond question, but his judgment in handling the Rivard case. Favreau promptly resigned as Minister of Justice, but Pearson persuaded him to stay on in the cabinet. He was, like Walter Gordon, a diminished politician.

The Rivard scandal cast its shadow over the rest of the year. While the Dorion inquiry was proceeding, in March 1965, Walter Gordon sent Pearson a memorandum calling for an election later that year. Gordon saw few risks and great potential advantage, as only a majority Liberal government could hope to pass desirable legislation. The quarrelsome Parliament elected in 1963 was no advertisement for the virtues of a house of minorities as far as the government was concerned. But would the electorate share the Liberals' exasperation? Some of Pearson's ministers thought not. Paul Martin in particular argued to the last against a 1965 election. But early in September Pearson decided to take the plunge and an election was set for November 8.

Gordon was anxious to have an election while Diefenbaker was still leader of the Conservative party. He and others

Small towns as well as large cities celebrated the centennial, sometimes in unusual ways. Bowsman, Manitoba (population 500) held this Centennial Privy Parade. *Public Archives Canada, C-30084.*

believed that Diefenbaker's reputation would be lethal to Conservative chances. They underestimated their opponent, for though Diefenbaker might be unable to win an election, he would not lose one either. Diefenbaker was a past master in the art of campaigning, and the Conservatives patched their party together for the occasion. Led by their "Chief," the

An exhibition train toured the larger cities, while exhibition caravans visited smaller centres and communities that could

not be included in the
train's schedule.
Public Archives Canada,
C-30083.

Tories garnered enough seats to preserve their position in
Parliament virtually intact. It was a notable, even if a negative,
triumph for Diefenbaker. Pearson won 131 seats, two short
of the tantalizing majority that he longed for.

As an immediate consequence, Pearson reshaped his
cabinet. Gordon, the architect of the election, resigned. Tom

Kent, Pearson's principal policy adviser, left to become Deputy Minister in a new Department of Manpower and Immigration. René Tremblay and Maurice Lamontagne, two ministers whose reputations had been touched by an unjustified scandal, were assessed as political liabilities and dismissed to make way for a "new look" cabinet. Pearson commented privately that "to force Ministers out of office in these circumstances was against my deepest instincts."

Most of the casualties of 1965 were from Quebec: Rouleau, Favreau, Tremblay and Lamontagne. Their demotions inevitably affected the morale of the Quebec Liberal caucus, and this in turn was a necessary backdrop to the next dramatic episode to mar Canadian politics: the Munsinger affair. This began with yet another cause célèbre, the case of George Victor Spencer, a Vancouver postal clerk who had provided the Soviet embassy with what he considered to be useful information. Spencer's activities as an amateur spy were discovered and he was dismissed from his government job, but not prosecuted, partly because the information he had conveyed had been unimportant and partly because he was known to be dying of cancer. Nonetheless, when word of this leaked out, the opposition managed to paint Spencer's case in bold black and white: either he was guilty and should be prosecuted, or he was innocent and should not have been penalized. The intervening grey area was left to the unlucky Liberals to defend. Grey is not a bright and attractive political colour, and the Liberals were soon losing the battle of political illusions. Behind the lines, Pearson reversed the government's position and there would be a judicial inquiry. Justice Minister Lucien Cardin, who had been valiantly assuring the politicians and the public that there was no need for an inquiry and that there would be no inquiry, was marooned. As Diefenbaker gloated in the House over the embarrassed minister, Cardin angrily replied that the leader of the opposition was "the very last person in the House who can afford to give advice on the handling of security cases in Canada." Baited further by Diefenbaker, the minister charged ahead: "I want the Rt. Hon. gentleman to tell the House about his participation in the Monseignor [sic] case when he was Prime Minister of this country."

Cardin's riposte to Diefenbaker occurred at precisely the point at which Pearson had lost control of his caucus. The memory of Conservative scandal charges rankled. The retreats, evasions and ruined careers of the past years infuriated the Liberal MPs. As the *Montreal Star* reported, Pearson came

"eyeball to eyeball with the caucus and his credentials of leadership were challenged." Unsuccessful efforts were made to muffle Cardin and to draw back before it was too late. Cardin held a press conference to clarify matters and before it was over, he had said enough to give the avalanche a final push. Another scandal was launched, and another royal com-

Public Archives Canada, C-25001.

COME ONE · COME ALL

TO THE

LIBERAL
PARTY

WEDNESDAY
OCT 27 · 8.00 p.m.

YORKDALE SHOPPING CENTRE

SEE!
19
PARADES
19

SEE!
MARCHING BANDS!
HUNDREDS OF
MUSICIANS!

SEE!
A GIGANTIC
FIREWORKS
DISPLAY!

SEE!
COLOURFUL
FLOATS!

**MEET THE
PRIME MINISTER
OF CANADA**

The Rt. Hon.
L. B. Pearson

COME BY CAR OR
TAKE THE DUFFERIN ST. BUS

160

mission had to be sent out in pursuit, this time headed by Mr. Justice Wishart Spence of the Supreme Court of Canada.

The principals and their lawyers marched off to a judicial inquest to hear the sordid story come out. Gerda Munsinger, an immigrant from East Germany whose father was believed to have taught in a German communist school in East Prussia before the war, pursued "an active career of prostitution" in Montreal. The RCMP learned that she was acquainted with Pierre Sévigny, Diefenbaker's Associate Minister of National Defence, with whom she had, in Mr. Justice Spence's words, a "liaison." Sévigny's official position was obviously a sensitive one and the situation posed the risk of a breach of security. When Diefenbaker was informed by the RCMP, he ordered Sévigny to stop seeing Munsinger, but took no further action. In the opinion of the Commissioner, he ought to have gone further: "It is difficult to understand how anyone could be retained in any Cabinet post when the slightest doubt remained as to his reliability from the point of view of national security." Sévigny's retention was described as "most imprudent." By the time the Spence report was released, in September 1966, Diefenbaker had characterized the Commission as a political inquisition designed to discredit him. Certainly the report did not help Diefenbaker, who was now facing the battle of his political life inside his own party.

On September 20, 1966, Dalton Camp, the president of the Progressive Conservative Association, called on both the major parties to reappraise their leadership in view of the uninspiring succession of scandals, charges, rumours and political vendettas that dominated the news from Ottawa. Camp denounced "the constant wounding of public men, the evasion of responsibility and the reluctance to face realities," over which Diefenbaker and Pearson had presided for the past couple of years. Camp could do little about Pearson, but he was prepared to confront his own leader. In the executive meeting of the Conservative Association in Ottawa in November, the national leader was heckled during his speech. Camp was re-elected as national president over the fierce opposition of the Diefenbaker forces, a victory which was confirmed by a call for a Conservative leadership convention to be held sometime in 1967.

The Conservatives met in Toronto in September. When the smoke cleared, Diefenbaker had been replaced as the Conservatives' national leader by Robert Stanfield, the craggy premier of Nova Scotia.

The old partnership of antagonism that dominated Cana-

OPPOSITE
Poster announcing a
Liberal rally in Toronto
during the election
campaign of 1965, in which
Pearson came within two
seats of winning a majority.
*Metropolitan Toronto
Library Board.*

Louis Riel, with music by Harry Somers and libretto by Mavor Moore, was one of the most successful cultural projects of the centennial year.
Canadian Opera Company.

dian politics since 1957 was dissolving. With Diefenbaker gone, it seemed appropriate for Pearson to go too. Pearson turned seventy in April 1967. Centennial year, with its cavalcade of international visitors and public events, was not an auspicious time to interrupt with Liberal party politics, and accordingly Pearson reserved his announcement of retirement until December. On December 14, he told his startled cabinet that "I've called a press conference for half an hour from now, at which I'm announcing my retirement from the leadership of the party." A leadership convention was to be called as soon as possible.

The cabinet and the party were initially dismayed by the sudden announcement, but soon aspirants for the leadership were enthusiastically touring the country soliciting support and votes. On one occasion in February 1968 so many members of the cabinet were absent (including Pearson, who was on vacation in Jamaica) that the government was defeated in a snap vote on a finance bill in the House of Commons. A highly disgruntled Prime Minister was forced to curtail his vacation and return to Canada to clean up the resulting mess.

Fortunately there wasn't much time left before the convention, and the Liberal candidates agreed to moderate their campaigning. A financial crisis came and went, helping to sink the leadership hopes of the Minister of Finance, Mitchell Sharp. Pearson remained officially aloof from the struggle, and as the Liberals' elder statesman he was warmly thanked for his services to the party. For two days, Pearson sat in his box in Ottawa's Civic Centre and watched the marching bands and listened to his colleagues' speeches as they strove to win the delegates' support. When Pierre Trudeau emerged victorious, Pearson joined him on the podium, and then headed for home. With the succession in hand, two weeks later he crossed Sussex Drive to Government House to hand in his resignation to the Governor General, his old friend and tennis partner Roland Michener.

6
Old Wine
in New Bottles:

A Canadian reconnaissance squadron, part of the UN peace-keeping force, encounters a solitary traveller in the Sinai desert. *Canadian Forces Photo.*

Canadian Foreign Policy Under Pearson

COMMONWEALTH PRIME MINISTERS' MEETING

Her Majesty Queen Elizabeth II with representatives of the Commonwealth countries at St. James's Palace, London

With the Queen are (back row, left to right): the Hon. D. B. Sangster, Acting Prime Minister of Jamaica; the Rt. Hon. Sir A. M. Margai, Prime Minister of Sierra Leone; the Hon. S. M. Kapwepwe, Minister of Foreign Affairs, Zambia; Brigadier Babate A. O. Ogundipe, Head of Delegation, Nigeria; the Hon. J. Murumbi, Vice-President of Kenya; His Beatitude Archbishop Makarios, President of Cyprus; Sardar Swaran Singh, Minister of External Affairs, India; the Hon. L. F. S. Burnham, Prime Minister of Guyana; the Hon. Sir Dawda Jawara, Prime Minister of The Gambia; the Hon. Dr. P. V. J. Solomon, Deputy Prime Minister and Minister of External Affairs, Trinidad and Tobago; the Hon. Lee Kuan Yew, Prime Minister of Singapore.

Front row (left to right): Mr. J. W. K. Harlley, Deputy Chairman, National Liberation Council, Ghana; Mr. Syed Sharifuddin Pirzada, Foreign Minister, Pakistan; Senator the Hon. A. F. Wijemanne, Minister of Justice, Ceylon; the Rt. Hon. Harold Holt, Prime Minister of Australia; His Excellency Ngwazi Dr. H. Kamuzu Banda, President of Malawi; the Rt. Hon. Harold Wilson, Her Majesty the Queen; the Hon. Dr. Giorgio Borg Olivier, Prime Minister of Malta; His Excellency Dr. A. Milton Obote, President of Uganda; the Rt Hon Keith Holyoake, Prime Minister of New Zealand; Tunku Abdul Rahman Putra Al-Haj, Prime Minister of Malaysia; the Rt Hon Lester B Pearson, Prime Minister of Canada.

From a photo panel prepared for British Information Services by the Central Office of Information, London, 1966. Laurier House. Public Archives Canada.

Two LIBERAL GOVERNMENTS came to power in 1963: the flesh-and-blood cabinet led by Pearson, and the ghost of the St. Laurent cabinet of 1957, rich in honours and achievements. In external affairs as in internal politics, the Canadian public expected, even demanded, a return to a comfortable sense of déjà vu.

The Liberals of 1963 were the self-conscious inheritors of a distinguished past. They could and did point to their capable direction of Canadian foreign policy between 1945 and 1957, a time when Canada enjoyed international respect and the favour of its allies. And Canadians were not alone in hoping that this happy time had come again. Pearson's friends abroad were delighted, and rejoicing in official Washington and London was barely concealed.

The mantle of external affairs passed to Paul Martin, Pearson's oldest acquaintance in the cabinet, and the foreign policy critic when the Liberals were in opposition. Martin had spent years preparing for the role of secretary of state for external affairs, as he had been a possible alternative for the job when Pearson had decided to enter politics. Martin too was an old League of Nations man, and had served on several Canadian delegations to the United Nations, where he had acquired a reputation as a skilled and patient diplomat.

Martin's promotion to external affairs was therefore a natural one. As an old Parliamentary hand, Martin had friends on all sides of the House. Even the opposition reluctantly admired his ability to say little at length when he judged the moment inopportune for candid revelation. But occasionally, commentators mistook the verbal fencing for the substance of inadequate policy, and damned the minister for a host of imaginary sins.

In fact, there was still general agreement inside and outside Parliament on what Canada's foreign policy should be. The cabinet, Parliament, and people in general believed that Canada should remain committed to the western camp, and should make the western alliance as strong as possible, i.e., as strong as public opinion in a peaceful decade would allow. The details of that job were left to Paul Hellyer, the new Minister of National Defence, a forceful and effective advocate of fuller participation in NATO.

First of all, the diplomatic details had to be squared away. On May 10, 1963, Pearson visited President Kennedy in his compound at Hyannisport, Massachusetts. Kennedy was widely admired in Canada as a super-politician, a young man of parts and promise. After the boredom of Eisenhower, the

President Kennedy at the UN in September 1963, just two months before his assassination. Left to right: Adlai Stevenson, US Ambassador to the UN; U Thant, Secretary-General of the UN; President Kennedy; Sosa Rodriguez (of Venezuela), UN Assembly President; Pearson, and Ralph Bunche, US Under-secretary for Special Political Affairs.
United Nations.

Americans had elected a comparatively young and certainly exciting man, who filled the airwaves with cadenced rhetoric urging commitment and challenge on his audience. When Kennedy has visited Ottawa in 1961, he had tried this out on Diefenbaker, only to meet a stony reception. Canadian-American relations had slid downhill thereafter, feeding Diefenbaker's suspicions that Kennedy's "New Frontiersmen" were in cahoots with Pearson's Liberals.

The 1963 visit was not the first meeting between Kennedy and Pearson, but it was the most successful meeting between a Canadian Prime Minister and an American President in several years. Differences were swept under the rug, harmony was restored, defence arrangements were once again set in motion. At the end of it all, Pearson emerged carrying the presidential flag as a symbol of solidarity.

Within seven months there was a new President. Kennedy was assassinated on November 22, 1963, and Pearson's next visit to the United States was to attend Kennedy's funeral in Washington. He spoke briefly with the new President, Lyndon B. Johnson, but postponed substantive discussion until a formal visit in January 1964 was made for the purpose of signing the latest agreement on the Columbia River. While Pearson and Johnson met frequently in the years that followed, their relations were never as warm as with Kennedy, and so too, Johnson was never as popular in Canada as his predecessor had been. Canadian-American relations passed quickly from spring to autumn without any intervening summer.

In the years that followed, Canadians gradually came to terms with a world in which their country was no longer an international factor of great importance. Far from having an assured voice in the councils of the world, Canada was beginning to scramble to make its voice heard at all. Confidence, shakily restored in the spring of 1963, was replaced with a nervous searching for "the Canadian role" in international affairs. The search for this "role" was complicated by the reluctance of the Canadian public to come to terms with international changes which it found uncongenial.

The most obvious change since 1957 was the virtually complete disappearance of the British Empire. It was not quite as though it had never been, since it left behind a Commonwealth that preserved and nurtured a combination of memories of a glorious monarchist past with dreams of a splendid multiracial future. It was as difficult to scotch fantasies about the recently deceased empire as to destroy the ludicrous optimism that many Canadians felt about their future as a leader of the former colonies in the Commonwealth. For a few years the Commonwealth even served as a surrogate for the wider world, for there Canada could still feel assured of prominence, even pride of place, as a rich and valued relative.

Events combined to disappoint the lavish hopes held out for the Commonwealth link. The member states disagreed with one another more often than not, and the principal purpose of the periodic Commonwealth meetings seemed to be to avoid public discord rather than to cultivate a genuine common interest. The Commonwealth, Canada's oldest international association and the strongest link with the past, was dying a slow, but painless and denatured death.

Nevertheless, Commonwealth meetings were still conducted with decorum and dignity. The United Nations was another matter. Both Pearson and Martin were strongly committed to the idea of a United Nations. For both it remained the best hope for mankind's future even though that future was an indefinite distance away. By the mid-1960s the automatic American majority in the United Nations was fading away. It was no longer possible to claim that the side of the majority was the side of the angels, unless one was inclined to believe that the angels disagreed with Canada, most of the time. However unpalatable the opinions of the emerging nations proved to be, Pearson and Martin understood their significance for the balance of world power, present and future. It would not be possible to hide in a western ghetto in an impoverished and antagonistic world.

Canadian interest in the United Nations was usually presented in more optimistic terms. There was the lingering memory of the Nobel prize, which endowed some journalists and academics with a sense of mission not generally shared outside Canada. The United Nations for the moment remained fashionable, and policies cast in its image — peacekeeping roles for the armed forces, for example — could be presumed to have greater appeal than the ordinary drudgery of defence. Canada's position at the United Nations remained co-operative, liberal and uncomfortable.

Peacekeeping was no empty word. The troops sent to the Sinai in 1956 were still there (not in person, of course) when Pearson returned to office. Under Diefenbaker Canadian troops had been sent to the former Belgian Congo (now Zaire) to help preserve some order in the midst of post-colonial chaos. When civil war threatened in the former British colony of Cyprus between the Turkish minority and the Greek majority, the United Nations formed another peacekeeping force and sent it to the island. Keeping the peace between Greeks and Turks on Cyprus also helped to keep the peace between Canada's NATO allies Greece and Turkey — a highly expedient and desirable goal.

When the United Nations troops, in their blue helmets, arrived in Cyprus in 1964, peacekeeping was viewed as a modest, but successful international activity. A few years later, Canadians had second thoughts. Since 1956 the United Nations troops in the Sinai had occupied certain strategic positions between Egyptian and Israeli forces. Of these, the most important were on the Straits of Tiran, overlooking the entrance to the Gulf of Aqaba, which gave access to Israel's southern port, Eilat. In the early part of 1967 relations between Israel and its Arab neighbours deteriorated rapidly. On May 17 the Egyptian government astonished the world

Shortly after Pearson became Prime Minister, President Kennedy invited him to visit him informally at Hyannisport. A cordial personal relationship resulted.
Public Archives Canada, C-90482.

with a demand that the UN troops on its soil be withdrawn from the Israeli frontier. This demand was expanded the next day into an order for the UN troops to quit Egypt altogether. The United Nations' Secretary General, U Thant, reluctantly agreed, and instructed the UN troops in Egypt to comply with the Egyptian order.

U Thant's decision was not favourably regarded in Ottawa. Pearson and Martin believed that the 1956 agreement, under which UN troops were stationed in Egypt, asserted a broad international interest in the maintenance of peace between Israel and Egypt, and that therefore Egypt could not

unilaterally abrogate its commitment. Martin publicly criticized U Thant's action, but the UN troops were removed
nonetheless.

Canada's protest at U Thant's surrender to Egypt found
little support and much abuse outside the western camp.
Egyptian president Nasser accused Canada of acting as a
stooge for the United States, and claimed that Pearson was
plotting aggression against Egypt. While Nasser was gas-
conading in front of Canada, the United States and Israel, the
Canadian troops were being hustled out of Egypt with little
notice and with considerable loss of equipment. Their hasty

and ungracious exit wounded Canadian self-esteem, and alienated support from future peacekeeping adventures.

With nothing standing between the Egyptians and the Israelis, the inevitable war followed. Within five days the Israelis were victorious on all fronts, and occupied the Sinai Desert right up to the Suez Canal. The Israeli victory was received with gratification in most western countries, including Canada. The war was interpreted as a struggle for Israel's survival, and possibly as a struggle against extermination of the Jews. John Diefenbaker expressed the opinion of most Canadians when he told the House of Commons that "Israel has a right to live."

In contrast to the aftermath of the Suez Crisis of 1956, the Middle East war of 1967 brought no satisfaction and scant hope. In fact, one strand of Canada's foreign policy — belief in and support for the United Nations — had very nearly come unravelled. The Egyptian rebuff to the UN and to Canada had blunted any desire to seek further nominal glory through foreign policy, and a mood of scepticism set in. Disillusionment was perhaps most marked outside the government, although even inside there was some disposition to question the reasonableness and even the feasibility of an active foreign policy. "Pearsonian diplomacy" was now an ailing growth.

A diminution in Canadian enthusiasm for an active foreign policy did not mean a diminution in the need for close attention to Canadian foreign relations. Housekeeping matters always needed attention, and housekeeping, unlike peacekeeping, was not a luxury. First on the agenda was the renegotiation of the Columbia River treaty of 1961. This treaty had been hurriedly signed by Diefenbaker and President Eisenhower in the expiring moments of the latter's term of office — a sentimental act which had unfortunate consequences. The terms of the treaty impinged on British Columbia's jurisdiction, and Premier W. A. C. Bennett decided that he was not satisfied. Some of the terms of the treaty therefore had to be renegotiated to meet British Columbia's objections, and eventually a solution that reconciled provincial politics with the national interest was reached. Many Canadians thought that the national interest was the loser in the deal, but without Bennett's consent there could be no effective treaty at all. In January 1964 Pearson and Johnson met to sign the supplemental agreement to the treaty.

This January 1964 meeting is better known for setting up a working group of officials to draft a statement of guiding principles for Canadian-American relations. Two distinguished

OPPOSITE
The opening of the new Toronto City Hall, one of the most remarkable buildings in Canada. Architecture left tradition far behind in the fifties and sixties.
City of Toronto Archives.

175

diplomats, Arnold Heeney from the Canadian side and Livingston Merchant from the American, were assigned to the task. Inevitably, the statement became known as the Merchant-Heeney Report. Heeney and Merchant investigated current or recent problems in Canadian-American relations, and tried to discover how they might have been better handled. They made specific recommendations on a practical level, and they also suggested general principles for governing Canadian relations with the United States, and vice versa. They commended "the practice of quiet diplomacy" as both "neighbourly" and "far more effective than the alternative of raising a row and being unpleasant in public." They pointed out the obvious truth that Canadian authorities were disposed to be sympathetic to American problems, although they also emphasized that this did not mean a derogation from Canadian independence.

All in all, it was an unexceptionable statement of platitudes, or so it must have seemed to its authors. It did not commend itself to vocal segments of Canadian opinion. Alvin Hamilton, Diefenbaker's former Minister of Agriculture, caricatured the report as a "diplomatic sell-out;" a columnist concluded that the report confirmed Canada's "lackey status," and even more moderate observers argued that the report committed Canada to keeping its opinion of American policy muted. The possibility that private speech might be an improvement on public hysteria got lost in the comments.

What the public reaction really signified, of course, was that American relations with Canada, and American foreign policy in general, were no longer as favourably viewed from Canada as in the 1940s or 1950s. These perceptions of American foreign relations were heavily influenced by reports on the American domestic scene, where the civil rights movement of the early 1960s was in full swing. Desegregation of schools, sit-ins for equal, shared facilities for blacks and whites, freedom marches in the American south, had a powerful impact on Canadian liberal opinion. Simultaneously, riots in northern American cities reminded Canadians that their forebears had perceived the United States as a violent society. For the most part Canadians saw the Americans' summers of unrest courtesy of American television, but in Windsor frightened citizens were able to watch smoke rising during riots in Detroit, just across the river. The prestige of the United States in Canada sank proportionately.

Almost unnoticed, in the mid-1960s an event occurred that put an end to one of the oldest characteristics of Canadian-American relations: the open border for immigrants heading south from Canada to the United States. Traditionally, the border between Canada and the United States had been a customs frontier, but where Canadian emigration was concerned, it had been generally open. Few old-stock Canadian families were without their American relatives and with every generation, more thousands of young Canadians headed south for money and opportunity. In 1965, however, the American immigration act was amended to regulate and limit the previously wholesale immigration from the western hemisphere. Henceforth, Canadian migration to the United States was more

Pearson and Johnson in the Oval Room of the White House, 1964. *Public Archives Canada, C-90375.*

President Johnson about
to sign the Autopact
agreement between
Canada and the US in
1965. Dean Rusk, US
Secretary of State, is on
the right.
UPI Photo.

geriatric than youthful in character, as older citizens sought
the sun in Florida or California.

The end of open immigration to the United States did
not become a significant irritant in Canadian-American relations. To the general surprise, a reverse movement soon began.
In the mid-1960s most Americans became conscious of two
facts about Canada: Canada did not have conscription for
military service, and it was not at war. The United States, however, was.

Since the early 1950s the United States had been support-
ing the anti-communist cause in Indo-China with supplies and
money, with military advisors, and finally with troops and air
power. This military intervention was concentrated in South
Viet Nam, whose army was proving more and more unable
to stand up to native guerrillas backed by North Viet Namese
troops. President Johnson therefore ordered American
ground forces into South Viet Nam, and sent the air force
to bomb the north.

It was not a propitious moment in Canadian-American
relations. Canadians already had their doubts about the United
States, and even previously accepted commonplaces, like the
desirability of American investment, were being steadily
undermined. The finance minister, Walter Gordon, was
known to look with disfavour on American domination of
the Canadian economy (as he perceived it to be), and although
Gordon himself was far from being an extremist, his advocacy
of Canadian economic nationalism found echoes much farther
to the left. Through the debate over foreign investment, anti-

178

Americanism and Canadian nationalism were fused into a powerful emotional combination.

Gordon's appeal was limited to certain groups. Less developed regions opposed any regulation of the flow of investment money, no matter what its source. Investment meant jobs to impoverished provinces far from rich metropolitan centres. Some even suggested that Gordon's nationalism was a peculiarly myopic expression of Toronto domination over the rest of Canada. It did not seem to make that much difference, outside Ontario, if new money came from Toronto or the United States. The difference, however, may have been that there was not as much of it from Toronto.

Even in Ontario, criticism of the economic preponderance of the Americans took second place to a trade treaty with the Americans: the Autopact of 1965. The agreement provided for a free interchange of automobile parts across the border, although with certain safeguards to preserve Canadian production. The Canadians, it was later recalled, would have preferred a wider agreement to cover chemicals and aircraft parts as well as cars, while the Americans believed that in signing the automobile pact they were anticipating far worse legislation from the Canadian government.

Pearson and Martin flew south again, this time to the LBJ Ranch where a wild and woolly reception awaited them. The atmosphere was congenial, if a little too informal for Pearson, and the talks were wide-ranging and highly informative.

A moment in Pearson's highly informal visit to President Johnson at the LBJ Ranch in 1965. *Public Archives Canada, PA-110818.*

It was Pearson's last altogether happy meeting with Johnson. The Viet Namese war was dragging on, with every operation transmitted back to the United States almost immediately for showing on the evening news. The brutality and the carnage of the war sickened many viewers, while the morality of the American cause failed to find plausible defenders. What started as a crusade against communism began to seem a struggle to shore up an unpopular indigenous dictatorship.

Canadian opposition to American involvement in Viet Nam began as early as 1965. With every escalation in the war, the ranks of dissent swelled. Canada's extreme left wing found confirmation for its theories as well as new sympathizers in the struggle against conspiratorial capitalism.

Pearson decided that it was time to make some kind of gesture and try to bring an end to the war through negotiation if possible. One frequently suggested avenue was the "bombing pause," the idea that if the Americans let up on their air offensive against North Viet Nam, negotiations could begin. Unfortunately the two sides had nothing to negotiate about.

Pearson's proposal for a pause in the Viet Nam bombing angered President Johnson, and it is doubtful if his departure for home was as cordial as this cartoon suggests. Its caption read "The thing that bothers me with Lester is that he always wants to make sense." *Bierman, Victoria* Daily Times. *Public Archives Canada, C-90436.*

The North Viet Namese wanted complete withdrawal of American troops, and the Americans wanted the North Viet Namese to leave South Viet Nam. Until one side or the other compromised, there was no obvious issue to any possible discussions.

Against the advice of his external affairs department, Pearson spoke at Temple University in Philadelphia, urging a pause in American bombing in the interests of peace. He was immediately summoned to a stormy interview with Johnson, who felt aggrieved and betrayed, and it is possible that Pearson's standing in Johnson's eyes was never the same thereafter.

The Temple speech was only the outward expression of Pearson's concern with the Viet Namese problem. Canada also had a toehold in Indo-China through its membership on the all but forgotten International Control Commission (ICC), a relic of the settlement of the first Indo-China war in 1954. As an ICC member, Canada had access to both sides of the lines, and traded on this unique status to sound the North Viet Namese about their attitudes to a settlement with the United States. Although these exchanges provided some interesting data, they were fruitless in the end.

Canada, in fact, had no leverage on either side. The war placed the Canadian government in an impossible moral dilemma in which it would have been extremely difficult to approve the aims or methods of either side, although there was certainly some pro-American (or perhaps anti-communist) sentiment among Canadians who had actually been to Viet Nam. There was no general disposition to quarrel with Canada's pro-American orientation in its over-all policy, either on the part of the government or in the public at large. Not all foreign policy commentators agreed. As far as they were concerned, Canadian foreign policy should more closely approximate to a strict standard of morality, and for them public evasions and silences were deplorable if not damnable.

Pearson was unable to satisfy either side. There was no room in the 1960s for the great initiatives of the 1940s. Then Canada, a rare, rich nation in the midst of poverty and chaos, had played a leading role in the post-war settlement and had enjoyed the trust and confidence of Britain and the United States. The times were not right in the 1960s for the same active Canadian policy. Optimism and commitment were transmuted into worry and indecision, as much on the public's part as on the government's. The sixties as far as Canadian foreign policy was concerned ended with a whimper.

7
"What Does Quebec Want?"

"CANADA," R. B. Bennett once remarked, "is one of the most difficult of all countries to govern." Macdonald and Laurier had said much the same thing before Bennett; Pearson could have said it after him.

One of the difficulties was the legacy of the British Conquest of 1760: two nations warring in the bosom of a single state, as Lord Durham put it in 1839. Since 1867 the two nations had dwelt together in a single federal state, segregating some of their most vital concerns in provincial compartments. Since then some English Canadians had formed the fixed conviction that Canada was simply a convenient excuse for French and Roman Catholic dominations, and some French Canadians believed just as firmly that Canada was a broad avenue leading to assimilation via subordination. But for the most part, the English and the French lived apart, in mutual ignorance and harmony, shielded by comforting and conflicting prejudices.

One such prejudice was the conviction that "nothing ever changes in the land of Quebec," an old quotation from the novel *Maria Chapdelaine*. The English-Canadian view of the French Canadians was consequently incorrigibly quaint, even when contrary evidence was daily presented. French Canada was still priest-ridden, as it had been in the 1860s. It was still basically rural, in character if not in statistics — an illusion shared in some quarters of Quebec. If French Canada changed at all, it would move toward the North American norm. It would acquire the spirit of progress and the faith in technology that typified the English-speaking majority in North America.

From the 1830s forward a few French Canadians had called for adaptation to some English ways. Education would be the key to equality. In the 1930s and 1940s isolated figures like the Liberal senator T. D. Bouchard were arguing for more

OPPOSITE
De Gaulle, then a popular figure in Canada, speaking to the crowd on Parliament Hill when he paid a wartime visit to Ottawa in 1944.
Public Archives Canada,
C-26947.

and better education and adaptation by French Canadians to the ways of the majority. They regarded this process as inevitable and they believed that it would be a happy process. From a similarity of circumstances would flow greater harmony and understanding between French and English Canada.

In the 1950s there were superficial signs that this would indeed be the case. Louis St. Laurent was a reassuring father figure for the whole country. Under his regime some talented French Canadians migrated to Ottawa to work for the federal government: men like the young Pierre-Elliott Trudeau, who worked in the Privy Council Office on the revision of the constitution, or, in a more senior position, Maurice Lamontagne, a Laval economist, who predicted a more liberal society in Quebec. Many Quebec intellectuals decried nationalism as an ideological hobgoblin that brought only isolation and ignorance in its train. In the aftermath of the Second World War, after all the excesses were committed in the name of the holy race or of the nation state, this position was easily understandable and hardly unreasonable.

Most English Canadians still thought of Quebec as a curious anomaly. When André Laurendeau, the editor of the Montreal newspaper *Le Devoir*, took a trip across Canada in the mid-1950s, he found a people whom he described as "very consciously Canadian but they don't realize that the Canada they dream of is an English Canada." When St. Laurent proclaimed that Quebec was a province like the others, he communicated different meanings to English and French Canadians. To English Canada, it was a message to Quebec to hurry up and get in step. To Quebec, if the idea was acceptable at all, it was an argument that a better life would be available — in French — from the Ottawa government.

Quebec was not, and had never been, impervious to the social changes going on outside the province. From the 1930s forward Quebec labour had been involved in a series of bitter strikes, just like labour in other provinces. But after 1945 labour troubles were more unsympathetically viewed in Quebec than in the other provinces. The history of labour-management relations in Quebec in the 1940s was a story of provincial intervention on the side of management. In the opinion of the provincial government, it was intervention on the side of industrial development and more investment in the province. In its underlying attitude the Quebec government was not different from the governments of other provinces. It simply carried it farther.

The most famous strike took place in the town of Asbestos in 1949. The local union went on strike against the international Johns-Manville corporation. The strike attracted support from Montreal (Trudeau and his friends Jean Marchand and Gérard Pelletier were there) and from the Roman

Maurice Duplessis, circa 1930.
Public Archives Canada, C-19522.

185

Catholic Church, although the bishops were not unanimous on the subject. The archbishop of Montreal, Mgr. Charbonneau, even informed his parishioners that "There's a conspiracy to destroy the working class, and it's the Church's duty to intervene!" Eventually the strike was settled. The working class was not destroyed (its destruction had never been intended) and the intransigent attitude of Duplessis' government had suffered a major setback.

Nevertheless, the government of Quebec remained in power. It behaved as governments of Quebec always had, and as some governments of other provinces sometimes did. Premier Duplessis maintained himself in office with the support of a plurality of the electorate over the ostentatiously "clean" opposition, the provincial Liberals. He beat the drum for provincial autonomy, for Quebec's traditions, for the old forms of society and authority, which Duplessis devoutly believed in. Behind him the Church came to heel (Archbishop Charbonneau was providentially exiled to Victoria, although not exclusively for his attitude in the Asbestos strike, as is often claimed).

Duplessis might have remembered the words of Canada's last French king, Louis XV: "Après moi le déluge." When Duplessis died in September 1959, the storm broke. An increasingly urban, middle-class society turned its face away from the old-fashioned nostrums of the nationalism of farm and parish. Quebec and its citizens were determined to make their way in a newer world. When Jean Lesage and his Liberal party narrowly defeated Duplessis' successor Antonio Barrette in June 1960, French and English Canada regarded the event as the beginning of a new era in English-French relations. How new, on-one as yet could guess.

Few at the time paid any attention to another event in 1960. In September some thirty people from Montreal, Hull and Ottawa met in a Laurentian resort and founded the Rassemblement pour l'Indépendance Nationale, the RIN. One of the RIN's spokesmen, Dr. Marcel Chaput, was promptly dismissed from the federal civil service. This time there were headlines. For the first time since the 1930s, separatism was discussed as a serious political possibility for Quebec, and for the first time it was not linked with one or the other of the exotic quasi-religious causes of the extreme right.

At first separatism had little direct impact on the course of provincial or federal politics. Within a short space of time, however, other and more powerful political forces began to converge in a line that seemed to lead directly towards a political division between Quebec and the rest of Canada. A political confrontation was in the making and the politically astute gradually became aware that not just the shape but the nature of Quebec and Canadian politics was changing.

The Conservative Party was the first to suffer from the changes in Quebec. Although Diefenbaker made his gestures of appeasement to Quebec opinion, these were regarded as changes of form rather than substance. The substance was the feeble representation of Quebec in the Diefenbaker cabinet, and that insured that Quebec would be ignored in Ottawa.

In the ordinary course of events, the Liberal party would have been the beneficiary of a Conservative decline. The Liberals had a long-established dominance in federal politics in the province, and could pick and choose among eligible and able candidates. The roster of Liberal candidates in 1962 and 1963 was impressive: Lionel Chevrier, one of the best debaters on the Liberal side of the House, and a former minister; Guy Favreau, the former Assistant Deputy Minister of Justice in Ottawa; Maurice Sauvé, director of public relations in Lesage's 1960 campaign; Jean-Luc Pépin, a bright and ambitious professor of political science; and, of course, the serried ranks of Liberal party backbenchers and party officials who provided the backbone of Liberal strength in Parliament. A belated member of the Quebec caucus, Maurice Lamontagne, elected on his third try in 1963, had also worked closely with Pearson in opposition.

One embarrassment for the Liberals was that none of the members from Quebec enjoyed an automatic predominance over the others. Chevrier was not from Quebec at all, to begin with, but was a Franco-Ontarian from Cornwall. Sauvé and Pépin were junior in the caucus and distrusted by more traditional politicians, and Favreau and Lamontagne lacked the political weight necessary to keep order among their colleagues. Despite their promise and their talents, the Liberals from Quebec presented a squabbling and disunited spectacle to the outside world.

But with all their deficiencies, these men were the best hope of the Liberals in dealing with Quebec. There were already indications that the stakes this time were not to be the ordinary ones of political advantage over the opposition, but the retention of Quebec inside the Canadian Confederation. As the 1963 election ground towards its indecisive climax, disturbing reports were received from Quebec: Molotov cocktails were tossed through the windows of federal armouries in Quebec; General Wolfe's statue in a Quebec City park was

Cardinal Paul-Emile Léger joins other dignitaries during the 1951 opening of the CBC building on Dorchester Street in Montreal.
Public Archives Canada, PA-77937.

toppled; and a bomb damaged a railway line over which Diefenbaker's campaign train was due to pass. A nearby barn had been painted with the letters FLQ.

It was the first public appearance of the Front de libération québecois. The name recalled, as it was meant to, the names of the various anti-colonial liberation movements that had grown up around the world, and it reminded Canadians that many of these movements had eventually succeeded in throwing out their colonial masters. English Canadians did not think of themselves as either conquerors or colonists in a strange and hostile land, but in Quebec there was a highly visible and relatively well-to-do English minority. The minority now began to feel notably less secure, particularly when the terrorists graduated from bombing property to bombing people, eventually killing an English-Canadian night watchman and crippling an army bomb disposal expert.

Opinion in Quebec was repelled by the terrorist bombs. Those responsible were soon rounded up and sent to jail. But the mere existence of a terrorist group altered the face of

Quebec politics, extending the political spectrum well beyond the respectable, verbal separatists of the RIN with their educational campaigns and their demonstrations. The unthinkable now moved into the realm of the possible.

The art of the possible, of course, is politics. A political problem like separatism cried out for a political solution, and Pearson, as the political head of the country, was responsible for finding one. His strategy was twofold. In July 1963 he established a Royal Commission "to inquire into and report upon the existing state of bilingualism and biculturalism in Canada and to recommend what steps should be taken to develop the Canadian Confederation on the basis of an equal partnership between the two founding races." Although the Commissioners' mandate instructed them to take other ethnic groups into account in their investigations and findings, the emphasis was squarely on French-English relations in Canada. As co-chairmen, Pearson appointed André Laurendeau, the editor of *Le Devoir*, and Davidson Dunton, a former president of the CBC then serving as president of Carleton University.

The Royal Commissioners immediately set to work, holding hearings, commissioning special studies, and then working on a preliminary report. This report, which appeared in February 1965, informed Canadians "that Canada, without being fully conscious of the fact, is passing through the greatest crisis in its history." The crisis, obviously, centred in Quebec. Its major symptom, if not its cause, lay in the fact that "the state of affairs established in 1867, and never seriously challenged, is now for the first time being rejected by the French Canadians of Quebec."

The form of rejection embodied in the FLQ impressed Canadians, who were not accustomed to think of their country as a scene of violence. But the FLQ could be dealt with by the ordinary methods of the police. It never achieved much direct support or sympathy in the population at large. The danger that the Royal Commissioners perceived was the disruption of Canada through ordinary political processes. In this political drama the participants were already on stage: the government of Canada and the government of Quebec.

In a play that enjoyed some currency in Quebec in the mid-1960s, "Hamlet, Prince du Québec," an actor wearing a Pearson mask played the part of Polonius, the verbose and unlucky counsellor to the King (English Canada). "Jean Lesage" played that of Ophelia, and "René Lévesque," his minister of resources, that of Horatio, the good friend to Hamlet who is, in this case, Quebec itself. The development of the play is

obvious: Hamlet-Quebec eventually does in Polonius-Pearson and Ophelia-Lesage, only to succumb to the treachery of the King (English Canada). Dying, Hamlet-Quebec passes the word to Lévesque-Horatio: "Vive le Québec libre."

Like the parody of Hamlet, the relations between Quebec and Ottawa often seemed to be tragedy reduced to the level of farce. Pearson and Lesage shared a common experience, the same party and a commitment to the preservation of the Canadian federal state. Both were men of uncommon ability, as well as successful politicians. Pearson hoped that Lesage might some day re-enter the federal cabinet where, in all probability, he could become leader of the national Liberal party and Prime Minister of Canada.

Unfortunately for Pearson and Lesage, the determinants of the politics of the 1960s did not allow for gentlemanly sparring between province and country. Lesage was the leader of the government of Quebec, but he was also the head of a cabinet of prima donnas who developed policies of their own in the name of the expanded jurisdiction of the Etat du Québec. Lesage discovered that being Maîtres chez nous did not imply being maître chez soi.

The Quebec premier's chief political dilemma, apart from containing a vigorous nationalist opposition under Daniel Johnson, was to seek a plausible reconciliation of Quebec's social and economic ambitions with Ottawa's political and economic predominance. Inevitably this meant that the federal government had to make some concessions to Quebec, and concessions to Quebec meant concessions to the other provinces. Thus the problem of resistance to Quebec separatism became entangled in the older problem of federal-provincial relations.

The basic Quebec position was elaborated by Lesage before the 1963 federal election. Quebec demanded greater "tax room." In effect, Ottawa was to tax less, and pay out less, so that Quebec might tax more and spend more on its own projects. The tax room could be created, it was believed, if the Ottawa government was prepared to vacate some of its shared programs with the provinces, or with Quebec alone. Lesage, in his discussions with federal ministers, discovered new ways to take advantage of equalization grants from Ottawa.

Sgt.-Major Walter Leja lies on the ground after being badly wounded by a bomb placed in a Montreal mailbox by separatists. *Montreal* Star—*Canada Wide.*

The justification for Quebec's demands in Pearson's and probably Lesage's mind was the expansion of Quebec's financial resources so that Quebec might undertake programs of its own in the social and economic realms. A delicate balance was involved. The federal government could not give up so much of its revenues and its powers that it became a secondary government with little ability to influence the national economy; the Quebec government must be seen to have enough power and money to achieve tangible objectives without the necessity of resorting to separatism. It was therefore necessary to make judicious concessions and then to be seen to be doing so. But as Pearson knew, appeasement could only go so far, and there was always the risk that Quebec's appetite for greater power would be whetted, not satisfied.

Pearson's approach was characteristically broadminded. "Co-operative federalism," that conveniently vague term, was the watchword invoked to cover and justify his general policy towards the provinces. Pearson abandoned some of his earlier faith in a strong central economic power, a legacy of his experience in the Depression of the 1930s, in order to grant the provinces more autonomy in their financial affairs. The strong image of Liberal centralization was replaced by the flexible one of Pearson's diplomacy, this time applied to the relations between the central government and the provinces. With enough good will, he hoped, anything was possible. "Indeed," Pearson commented in 1966, "my whole career, my deepest instincts, have been dedicated to the resolution of disputes, to the search for agreement, to the avoidance of controversy and to find solutions to difficult problems." As one observer stated, "It was a whole new world when Pearson came in."

The avoidance of controversy sometimes looked rough when contemplated through the concentrating focus of a television screen. Canadians were treated to the spectacle of crisis negotiations, fist-pounding, harsh words and inflexible rhetoric. Headlines recorded the lurching progress of interminable federal-provincial conferences towards some kind of agreement, made possible at the last moment by a judicious change of front on the part of some or all of the participants.

Agreement could not always be secured, however. One of Pearson's objectives was the complete repatriation (or patriation, since it had never dwelt in Canada before) of the constitution. St. Laurent had managed to secure for the federal Parliament the power of amending those sections of the British North America Act applying to the federal government alone. Now it was for the next Liberal Prime Minister to complete

his work by securing agreement on an amending formula which would allow all sections of the Canadian constitution to be amended in Canada.

Lesage agreed with Pearson. An attempt at working out a formula had been made by the Conservative justice minister, Davie Fulton. Guy Favreau, his Liberal successor, took up the Fulton formula. It was discussed at a federal-provincial conference in Charlottetown in September 1964, the hundredth anniversary of the first Charlottetown conference that laid the groundwork for Confederation. Under the sunny influence of compromise, the premiers agreed that the Canadian constitution should be repatriated, and that the basis should be the formula worked out by Fulton in 1961. Or, as the end-of-conference communiqué stated, they agreed "in principle." A world of difference lay between principle and practice. The Fulton formula, now dubbed the Fulton-Favreau formula, attempted to solve the conundrum of amending a constitution without offending regional or racial minorities by requiring unanimous consent of the provinces to amendments that affected provincial powers or property, or the use of the English or French languages.

This seemed to break the logjam of decades. In English

The Pearsons with Georges Pompidou (then Premier of France) and Madame Pompidou in Paris in 1964.
Public Archives Canada, PA-110784. Capital Press.

Canadian National's spectacular turbo train speeding through the Ontario countryside. When Pearson joined Mackenzie King's cabinet in 1948, Canadian railways were still purchasing steam locomotives. By the time he became Prime Minister the diesel was King of the Rails. By the time he retired, CN was preparing to introduce the turbo train — a high-speed, low-slung, streamlined train of revolutionary design. It had its teething troubles, but soon was providing a swift service between Montreal and Toronto — the busiest and most lucrative section of the 715-mile corridor from Quebec City to Windsor on which the railway has the best prospect of competing successfully with other modes of transportation. Mid-town arrivals and departures are still attractive, and growing congestion at airports makes them even more so. *CN Photo.*

Canada there was some questioning of the federal government's strategy in seeking a compromise solution by entrenching an extreme provincial rights position. "It could be a milestone in the break-up of Confederation," the *Toronto Star* intoned. Pearson even had some difficulty in defending the agreement inside the Liberal caucus and the cabinet. The Conservatives naturally scented blood, and promptly reversed their initial position of critical approval. Despite a memorandum from Fulton explaining that the Charlottetown agreement was virtually identical with the Conservative proposal of 1961, Diefenbaker went out to bust the damn thing.

Criticism outside Quebec concentrated on the clause in the agreement that permitted a re-allocation of powers between the federal and provincial governments. Such an exchange of powers would in fact, if not in theory, create a distinct status for Quebec, which could become an associate state rather than a true member of Confederation. But it was the reaction inside Quebec that mattered. The Union Nationale opposition argued that the agreement would have the effect of freezing Quebec's constitutional status; far from establishing an associate status for Quebec, it would prevent such a development. Johnson bluntly accused Lesage of "treason" to Quebec. Lesage tried to mobilize support behind the Charlottetown formula, but it was too late. A resolution approving the federal-provincial agreement was promised but never introduced. Quebec opinion was apparently not prepared to consent to any arrangement that might reinforce "the state of affairs established in 1867." If anything was necessary to confirm the Bilingualism Commission's diagnosis of a Canadian crisis, it was the failure of the Fulton-Favreau formula.

Lesage's abandonment of the formula coincided with the decline of Favreau's own position in Ottawa. By 1965 Ottawa had become a graveyard for the reputations of Pearson's Quebec ministers. His government was weakened thereby, and Pearson's ability to represent Quebec to the rest of Canada, and the rest of Canada to Quebec, was diminished. Favreau's eclipse ironically opened the way to an unexpected development. For some time Favreau, in his capacity as leader of the Quebec federal Liberals, had been negotiating with Jean Marchand, the president of the Quebec-based Confederation of National Trade Unions, with an eye to his entry into federal politics. The major obstacle was Marchand's wish to bring some of his friends with him: Gérard Pelletier, one of Quebec's best-known journalists, and Pierre-Elliott Trudeau, law professor and editor of the magazine *Cité Libre*. It was Trudeau who had called Pearson the "defrocked pope of peace" in 1963, and many Liberals had neither forgiven nor forgotten. Both Trudeau and Pelletier were generally assumed to be closer to the NDP than to the Liberals.

Pearson was not one to hold a grudge. When Maurice Lamontagne told him of the discussions with Marchand, Pelletier and Trudeau, he was delighted. He was willing to admit, as he later wrote, that "I was right and they were wrong." Now they could begin again. The attraction of "the three wise men," as they were soon called, was that they were already men of standing in their province, neither connected with nor tainted by the old politics. All three agreed to run in the federal election of 1965 in order to reinforce the cause of federalism in their province. When the three were victorious, Marchand was appointed to the cabinet, and Trudeau was given the post of Parliamentary Secretary to the Prime Minister, an office which in Pearson's opinion did not give him very much to do "nor the opportunity to learn very much." But their association was amicable and when Lucien Cardin retired as Minister of Justice in 1967, Trudeau was appointed to succeed him.

The Liberals needed all the help they could get. In 1966 Jean Lesage led the provincial Liberals to the polls in Quebec. To general surprise and Lesage's stupefaction, the Liberals lost to Daniel Johnson's Union Nationale. They managed to retain a plurality of the popular vote, a fact which Johnson dismissed by noting that the Union Nationale had won a majority of the French language vote. This seemed a bad sign for the future.

Oddly, however, relations between Ottawa and Quebec City were not much worse on the surface under Johnson than they had been under Lesage. Pearson and Lesage were friends and shared, broadly, the same objectives. It was not easy for Pearson to negotiate with Lesage as an adversary. Lesage, on the other hand, had to present his meetings with Pearson as dramatic confrontations to avoid the suspicion of being an Ottawa stooge. Johnson was a distinct contrast to Lesage. He was calm, where Lesage was emotional, sedate where Lesage was flamboyant. Meetings with Johnson, however, showed a tendency to degenerate into exchanges of friendly platitudes, and concrete results proved harder to come by. Pearson later wrote that he believed that Johnson had a real "desire for a united Canada with a contented Quebec," but it is difficult to conclude that that objective was much advanced through their relations.

By the time Johnson came to power, the federal government had made very sizeable concessions to Quebec and the other provinces. In 1963, Ottawa returned 9 per cent of corporation taxes, 17 per cent of income taxes and 50 per cent of succession duties, collected within each province, to the provincial government. In addition, since 1957, the federal government had been making formal payments to equalize the provinces' capacity to participate in various social welfare schemes. Under equalization, Quebec, which was considered to be a below average province in terms of tax revenue, secured significant grants from the federal government. As Quebec withdrew from certain shared cost programs, it received an abatement on income tax collected within the province. By 1968, Quebec's tax room amounted to 50 per cent of corporation taxes, 10 per cent of the personal income tax, and 75 per cent of succession duties. In the opinion of many Canadians, it was enough. In the opinion of some within the province, it was still too little. And for some of those it would remain too little until Quebec collected 100 per cent within each category, and only complete independence could guarantee that.

When finance minister Mitchell Sharp, Gordon's successor, met the representatives of the provinces in the fall of 1966, he informed them that the great giveaway was over. The federal government intended to take a final settlement of provincial claims by getting out of more shared-cost programs. After giving the provinces the monetary equivalent of the programs abandoned by the federal government, they would refuse to give any more. If the provinces wished to raise further revenues for their own purposes, they would have to take the responsibility for it before their own electorates, rather than leaving the federal government to face the voters' wrath alone.

The refusal of the latter to play the old game by the old rules came as a disappointment to the provincial premiers, and to none more than Daniel Johnson. Although Johnson launched his rhetorical weapons at the federal position, he could do little at that juncture. And the quarrel between Quebec and Ottawa took an unexpected turn, passing from the financial field to the international.

When the last French troops sailed away from Canada in 1760, the Franco-Canadian relationship was effectively shattered, and although tenuous links persisted through the next two centuries, they did not restore that relationship to a generalized, harmonious level. In the twentieth century Cana-

Pearson addressing the
Liberal Convention in
Ottawa that elected Pierre
Elliott Trudeau who was to
succeed him as leader in
April 1968. The tilt of the
head when speaking was
characteristic.
Public Archives Canada.

"Trudeaumania" swept the country when Trudeau campaigned in the general election of 1968, which gained him the majority that Pearson never enjoyed. He appears in the centre of this photograph, but is so hemmed in by admirers that he can scarcely be identified.
Public Archives Canada.

dian troops had fought in France in two world wars, while France, like other European countries, received Canadian economic aid at the end of the Second World War. During that war Canada, and Pearson, had taken a sympathetic attitude to the efforts of General Charles de Gaulle's liberation committee, in spite of the frequently expressed disapproval of the American government. When Pearson first met de Gaulle, in 1944, he found the French general both kind and sympathetic. American reports that the general was basically anti-Anglo-Saxon he dismissed. In some respects, he reported to Ottawa, de Gaulle's opinions on foreign policy were preferable to the Americans'.

Time passed. In 1964 Pearson and Martin visited Paris to meet President de Gaulle. Circumstances had changed since 1944. De Gaulle was now head of state and an effective head of the government of a powerful and proud nation. His intention was to assert French power and prestige as against the Anglo-Saxon powers that had directed the western alliance since 1945. Pearson's interview with de Gaulle was, in his opinion, friendly, but nevertheless intimidating – he faced "a large President . . . in a very large chair."

The large President and the small Prime Minister did not meet again. At first, it seemed that tranquillity would be preserved. Regrettably, Canada's position as a close economic partner and political ally of the United States coloured de Gaulle's opinion of Canada, and confirmed his view that Canada was just another, smaller, Anglo-Saxon nation. The rise of Quebec nationalism evidently intrigued de Gaulle, as it did many Frenchmen, especially because along with Quebec's economic and cultural assertions, there came a demand for a closer association with France. This association, if it was to exist on a diplomatic level, presumed some co-operation from Ottawa, since direct diplomatic relations are restricted to sovereign states. The Quebec government seemed to be more than willing to assume such a position for itself, and the resulting divergence between Ottawa and Quebec was barely papered over by a so-called "umbrella agreement" conceding direct relations between Quebec and France on cultural and educational matters.

When Canada's centennial year rolled around the stage was set for a political explosion. To celebrate the centennial, Queen Elizabeth and foreign heads of state from the Shah of Iran to the King of Thailand visited Canada. Among them was President de Gaulle. By the time the French leader had arrived on Canadian soil Pearson had noticed some disturbing signs.

OPPOSITE
De Gaulle on the balcony of the Hôtel de Ville in Montreal in 1967, where he startled and infuriated Pearson by shouting the slogan of the separatists: "Vive le Québec libre!" *Public Archives Canada, C-6013.*

The Quebec government knew more about de Gaulle's plans and movements than did Ottawa, although the Canadian government was the official host. Conflicts arose between federal and provincial officials over de Gaulle's precise itinerary. The federal presence in welcoming de Gaulle in Quebec City was treated as a scarcely tolerable inconvenience.

These were, perhaps, minor matters, but worse was to come. On July 24 de Gaulle drove, as scheduled, from Quebec City to Montreal. In Montreal, he was met by a wildly enthusiastic crowd in front of the city hall. He proceeded to address the crowd and his speech was carried on national television. Pearson, watching the news on his television, gaped incredulously as de Gaulle concluded his emotional harangue by shouting the slogan of the Quebec separatists, "Vive le Québec libre!"

Although at the best of times de Gaulle's intervention would have raised a storm, in July 1967 it coincided with the euphoric nationalism aroused by the centennial celebrations. And so it became not simply a hostile political gesture but an affront to all of Canada. Liberal ministers were deluged with the outraged reactions of thousands of ordinary Canadians. Even if the cabinet had wanted to minimize the incident it would have been politically suicidal to do so. It held two meetings on July 25, and the overwhelming preponderance of opinion favoured an immediate forceful reply.

Pearson was especially indignant at de Gaulle's choice of an analogy to illustrate his feelings in travelling through Quebec. When de Gaulle had addressed the crowd in Montreal, he told them that "I want to tell you a secret: this evening I find myself in an atmosphere like that at the Liberation." The liberation of France was familiar to some thousands of Canadian troops who had fought and died for it in two world wars, and to have their achievement flung back in Canada's face was more than Pearson could bear. The reply from the federal Cabinet was short and blunt. De Gaulle's words of the previous evening were "unacceptable to the Canadian people and its government." The statement continued:

> The people of Canada are free. Every province of Canada is free. Canadians do not need to be liberated. Indeed, many thousands of Canadians gave their lives in two world wars in the liberation of France and other European countries.
>
> Canada will remain united and will reject any effort to destroy her unity.

When de Gaulle received the rebuff, which could hardly have

been unexpected, he cancelled the remainder of his visit, which would have included a trip to "federal Canada" in Ottawa, and returned home.

He left behind a furore of mutual misunderstanding and bitterness between English and French Canadians. French Canadian editorialists viewed the furious English Canadian reaction as yet another manifestation of English bigotry, and tended to minimize the provocation offered by the general. English Canadians were startled to discover that French Canada was not much offended by what seemed to be a blatant intervention in internal Canadian affairs by a foreign head of state.

It is still unclear what de Gaulle expected to accomplish by crying out "Vive le Québec libre." In his subsequent comments and actions he left no doubt of his hostility to Canada, as he predicted that Quebec would indeed manage to shake off centuries of Anglo-Saxon oppression. Over the next few years Quebec's official visitors to France were showered with honours and attention, while the representatives of Canada languished in obscurity. But de Gaulle's intervention in Canadian affairs remained largely verbal. If words alone could effect a change in Canada's political balance, de Gaulle indeed did his best, or worst. But French encouragement of Quebec separatism did not go much farther than words and nuisance gestures.

The main adversary was at home, not in France: Daniel Johnson, not de Gaulle. The Quebec government was committed to seeking a revision of the Canadian constitution, to seeking, in Johnson's phrase, "equality or independence." Equality, the more palatable option, was left undefined, meaning all things to all men, a matter of some convenience to the Union Nationale party, which spanned the political spectrum from federalism to separatism. It began to seem as if some form of constitutional negotiation must take place, if only to satisfy Quebec's minimum demands.

A constitutional conference could not be bilateral. As matters stood, all provinces would have to be invited to such a conference, and most provinces did not put constitutional revision very high on their lists of priorities. The key province, Ontario, took a different view. Premier John Robarts had become concerned over Quebec's increasing isolation from the other provinces and from English Canada in general, and tried to defuse a possible confrontation between English and French Canada by holding a "Confederation of Tomorrow" conference in luxurious surroundings in Toronto. There, basking in the atmosphere of compromise and the anticipation of Christmas, the premiers got along rather better than expected. Johnson was unusually conciliatory and stressed the common ground between the provinces, rather than their differences.

With this feast of concord behind them, the provincial premiers prepared for their next conferences, which, unlike the inter-provincial meeting in Toronto, would be held under federal auspices in Ottawa, in February 1968. Issues of substance would be discussed, and there was room for disagreement. Since the debates were to be televised, there was a possibility that there would be a true constitutional debate staged for the benefit of the Canadian public.

Pearson was both host and president of the conference. Although he was of course committed to the federal position, his function as chairman predisposed him to avoid controversy with the premiers. Years of dramatized quarrels and negotiations in international and federal-provincial diplomacy had prepared him for this. The effective presentation of the federal case was left to the Minister of Justice, Pierre-Elliott Trudeau. He was a strong believer in the existing balance of powers in the Canadian constitution, arguing that present arrangements gave the provinces all necessary powers for cultural and social development. The idea that Quebec wanted more, or really needed more, to get "particular status," deeply offended him. "I think that particular status for Quebec is the biggest intellectual hoax ever foisted on the people of Quebec and the people of Canada," Trudeau stated.

The inevitable verbal combat between Ottawa and Quebec, between Trudeau and Johnson, took place on schedule. Johnson declared that the only way to keep Quebec in Confederation was to give its provincial government greater powers. Trudeau countered by saying that a diminution in the powers and responsibilities of the federal government would cut the links between Ottawa and the ordinary citizen, creating a separatism in fact, if not in theory. What was building to a bitter exchange broke off when Pearson called a providential coffee break.

The constitutional conference of 1968, which dissolved with promises to meet again, was Pearson's last major public function. In Trudeau's resistance to Johnson's claim to speak for Quebec, fundamental issues had emerged to divide the two parties. Diplomacy could postpone the confrontation in the hope that it would cool off, or that something better would turn up.

In the opinion of the admiring television audience, and of the press covering the conference, something already had. The handsome young justice minister was a breath of novelty in Canadian politics. At the time of the conference Pearson had already announced his intention to retire and the leadership race was in full swing. None of the Liberal hopefuls had the

The Rassemblement pour l'Indépendance Nationale (the RIN) demonstrating at the time of de Gaulle's visit to Quebec in 1967. *Public Archives Canada, C-5306.*

good fortune to secure the fortuitous exposure that Trudeau had received.

Trudeau was not Pearson's first choice for the succession. Over the years he had had several alternative leaders in mind. When he decided to retire he turned first to Jean Marchand,

The "Three Wise Men" from Quebec lunching at the Prime Minister's residence, 24 Sussex Drive: Jean Marchand, Pierre Trudeau and Gérard

PEARSON ENJOYED precisely one day as a private Member of Parliament. On April 23, 1968, Pearson's seventy-first birthday, Prime Minister Trudeau dissolved Parliament and appealed to the people for a majority Liberal government. He got it, as Canada was swept by Trudeaumania. On June 25, election day, Trudeau watched the results on television with the Pearsons in the Chateau Laurier in Ottawa.

Although Pearson had the stature of an elder statesman, he had no formal duties as such. There was his "rose-covered cottage" in Rockcliffe, Ottawa's refuge for diplomats and retired civil servants. There was a variety of offers of visiting professorships, including one from Harvard University. The most attractive offer, however, came from Robert McNamara, the president of the World Bank in Washington.

In August 1968 McNamara announced that Pearson would head a Commission on International Development for the Bank. The Commission's mandate was to study the impact of several decades of international aid on the underdeveloped world. The aid had been given in the hope of relieving and possibly curing the chronic poverty that afflicted Latin America and post-colonial Asia and Africa. With some exceptions, the aid had had little or no permanent impact. Meanwhile, in the late 1960s, developed nations were paying more attention to the complaints of their taxpayers, who grumbled about the ceaseless flow of good money after bad in apparently futile, if well-intentioned, projects. Pearson, when Prime Minister, had presided over a substantial increase in Canada's foreign aid. Now, with his commission, he had an opportunity to assess the results.

Pearson's commission was not without its difficulties. A majority of the commissioners represented the developed nations, the aid-givers, a situation which was understandably resented by the recipient countries, who aired their feelings on the matter as the commission toured the world. Public disagreements were a familiar problem to a veteran of federal-provincial conferences. When necessary, Pearson's talent for compromise, his charm and good nature, all came into play. In the end, agreement was secured. When the commission's report, *Partners in Development*, was published in October 1969, its very existence testified to Pearson's influence, although he had actually written only the first chapter. The report argued that as a matter of humanity, international aid should be continued and increased, and, sensibly enough, it suggested that partnership between donors and recipients was the only rational way to make aid succeed.

OPPOSITE
Pearson's study in his Ottawa home. Note the reproduction of the new Canadian flag in the rug in front of the desk.
Public Archives Canada,
C-90348.

Three Prime Ministers
are guests at John
Diefenbaker's seventy-fifth
birthday party.
CP Photo.

With his report completed, Pearson turned to two new projects: a return to his interrupted academic career through a professorship at Carleton University, and the composition of his memoirs. University seminars were no problem after cabi-

Certificate accompanying the Order of Merit awarded to Pearson by Queen Elizabeth. *Public Archives Canada*, C-94166.

nets. Students were impressed by Pearson's friendly and down-to-earth approach. As Pearson settled into the routines of teaching, he began work on his memoirs. More publicly, he also gave some attention to another long-term love: sports. He became honorary chairman of Canada's first major league baseball club, the Montreal Expos, visited their training camp in Florida, and was even assigned a locker.

The publication of the first volume of Pearson's memoirs, inevitably and appropriately called *Mike*, was a major literary event. Within a week they were a best seller. Shortly thereafter, however, Pearson got bad news from his doctors. In 1963, Pearson had had an operation for the removal of a benign growth near his ear. In 1970, he had another operation, and lost an eye to cancer. Now, just as the memoirs were fully underway, he learned that the cancer had spread. Abandoning all other projects, he spent six weeks working on his memoirs,

OVERLEAF
On a dreary winter day plagued by freezing rain, the funeral procession nears the remote little cemetery in the Gatineau Valley where Pearson was laid to rest beside his friends and colleagues, Hume Wrong and Norman Robertson. *CP Photo.*

and then went to Florida for a vacation. He collapsed, and was hastily flown back to Ottawa on Christmas Eve. There, on December 27, with his wife and children at his bedside, he died.

On December 30, 1972, Pearson's body lay in state in the Hall of Honour in the centre block of the Parliament Buildings in Ottawa, guarded by four officers of the unified armed forces. His medals and awards, including the Order of Merit from the Queen, his Nobel Prize medal, and the Order of Canada, were placed beside the coffin. Over twelve thousand people braved a blizzard to pay their last respects. The next day, the funeral service was held in the Anglican Christ Church cathedral a few blocks from the Parliament Buildings. The family, the cabinet, and various foreign dignitaries led by the British Prime Minister, attended.

After the service, family members and a few close friends accompanied the coffin to a little cemetery in the Gatineau Hills, north of Ottawa. There, in a second howling blizzard, Pearson was laid to rest beside his friends and colleagues, Hume Wrong and Norman Robertson.

Pearson's death brought a flurry of assessments and re-assessments. Whatever disagreements Pearson had occasioned in his public capacity were forgotten as colleagues and critics paid tribute to him as a man. Judy LaMarsh, who had roasted Pearson in her memoirs, told the press that she doubted "if there was anyone who ever hated him." "He may have had failings as a Prime Minister or as a leader," she continued, "but he had few failings as a human being." There was no dissent on that score.

The curious dichotomy between the public Pearson and the private man will likely never be resolved. For all his at-tractive public qualities, Pearson kept a large part of himself in reserve, as Arnold Heeney had remarked twenty years be-fore. His cheery informality and his open friendliness some-times led people to believe that he sympathized with them more than was really the case. Occasionally, too, his reluctance to become involved in public slanging matches disappointed his colleagues, who complained that he lacked some of the attributes of a leader.

Certainly Pearson never achieved the reputation of being a master of the political arts. He never received the grudging respect accorded to Mackenzie King, with his reputation for infallible judgment and brilliant timing. Nor was he seen as a great warrior on the hustings, as Diefenbaker was. In the sphere of political drama, Pearson was a failure. But as Prime

Minister, he was called on to run a craft shooting the rapids — with rocks, waterfalls, hidden branches and treacherous eddies. Mere survival implied formidable powers of navigation.

When Pearson handed on Canada to his successor, it was scarcely recognizable as the placid country of his youth. In the course of a lifetime, many familiar signposts had disappeared utterly. As Prime Minister, Pearson had had to find new directions while reassuring his countrymen about the old ones. From him, they accepted it, at least in part because, as one friend put it, he was "so utterly likeable a person."

Bibliography

ANY FURTHER READING on Pearson must start with his own memoirs, *Mike*, published in three volumes between 1972 and 1975 (Toronto, University of Toronto Press). Of these, only the first volume was completed by Pearson before his death, and it provides an excellent sample of Pearson's affable prose, although it is less satisfactory as a guide to the diplomatic issues with which he dealt. Volumes two and three, which are composites of Pearson's own early drafts for his memoirs and of contemporary documents, such as diary entries, are less pleasurable reading and are inevitably spotty and episodic in their coverage of Pearson's life and times. Nevertheless, there is a great deal of valuable material in them.

There are also several collections of Pearson's speeches, of which the best is *Words and Occasions* (Toronto, University of Toronto Press, 1970). Before and after his death, Pearson was memorialized by biographers and essayists: Robert Moon, *Pearson: Confrontation Years against Diefenbaker* (Hull, High Hill Publishing House, 1963) is of little importance. John Beal's *The Pearson Phenomenon* (Toronto, Longmans, 1964) is better, and contains a fair amount of personal material. W. Burton Ayre's *Mr. Pearson and Canada's Revolution by Diplomacy* (Montreal, Harvest House, 1966) is a peculiar book, marred by its uncritical admiration for its subject. The journal of the Canadian Institute for International Affairs, *International Journal*, published a special issue, *Lester Pearson's Diplomacy*, of articles of distinctly varying merit. In 1975 Michael G. Fry edited a collection of essays in honour of Pearson, *Freedom and Change* (Toronto, McClelland and Stewart, 1975), of which the best is by one of Pearson's former colleagues, Escott Reid, "Canada and the Creation of the North Atlantic Alliance, 1948-1949." Valuable for Pearson's years in retirement is a biography by Bruce Thordarson,

Lester Pearson, Diplomat and Politician (Toronto, Oxford University Press, 1974). For future scholars, the Pearson Papers in the Public Archives of Canada in Ottawa, when opened, will be a major source; only those papers dealing with the period down to 1948 have been consulted for this volume.

Two of Pearson's colleagues have written their recollections of their cabinet service. Judy LaMarsh, in *Memoirs of a Bird in a Gilded Cage* (Toronto, McClelland and Stewart, 1968) and Walter Gordon, *A Political Memoir* (Toronto, Macmillan, 1977). Both present a fairly jaundiced view of Pearson's dealings with his cabinet and party. Of interest for the Conservative side are two volumes of interviews edited by Peter Stursberg, *Diefenbaker: Leadership Gained* (Toronto, University of Toronto Press, 1975), and *Diefenbaker: Leadership Lost* (Toronto, University of Toronto Press, 1976). Diefenbaker has written his own memoirs, *One Canada* (three volumes, Toronto, Macmillan, 1975-77), but they are both verbose and trivial.

Index